Contents

DEEP FRIED UNLEAVENED BREAD (POORI)

Serves: 4-5 **- Preparation Time:** 20 minutes **- Cooking time:** 15-20 minutes

INGREDIENTS

- Ghee or oil for deep frying

For dough:

- 2 cups wheat flour (atta)
- 1 teaspoon salt
- 2 tablespoons semolina (optional)
- 1 cup water

DIRECTIONS

1. Mix the dry ingredients for the dough.
2. Add water a little at a time while kneading. The resulting dough should be slightly stiff.
3. Divide the dough into about 12 parts of equal sizes.
4. Roll each piece into a ball and flatten into small circles using a rolling pin. Arrange them on a tray and cover with a towel to keep the dough from drying out.
5. Heat the oil or ghee for deep frying. Test the oil by dropping in a small piece of dough. The oil is hot enough if the dough steadily floats to the surface. If it doesn't, the oil isn't hot enough. If the dough rises too rapidly, the oil is too hot.
6. Fry the poori one at a time. Press down gently with a ladle or slotted spoon. The poori will puff up. Flip over and fry until golden brown.
7. Take the fried poori out and drain on paper towels.
8. Serve hot with curry or sweet dishes.

INDIAN FLATBREAD (NAAN)

Serves: 4-6 **- Preparation Time:** 2 hours (includes resting and proofing of dough) **- Cooking time:** 30 Minutes

INGREDIENTS

- 1 tablespoon sugar
- ½ teaspoon instant yeast
- 1 cup water or as required
- 3 cups wheat flour (atta), divided
- 3-4 tablespoons yogurt
- 2 tablespoons butter, softened or ghee

- ¾ teaspoon salt
- Sesame seeds or nigella seeds/onion seeds (kalonji), optional

DIRECTIONS

1. In a medium bowl, combine the sugar, yeast, and water. Stir.
2. Add 1 cup of the wheat flour and stir to make a dough.
3. Cover and let rest for 40-45 minutes.
4. Add the remaining flour, yogurt, butter and salt.
5. Knead into a smooth dough. Adjust the consistency by adding a little flour (if too sticky) or water (if too dry).
6. Place it in a bowl, cover, and let it rise for 25 to 30 minutes.
7. Divide the dough evenly (about 12-14 pieces) and roll it into balls. At this point, you may sprinkle some sesame or nigella seeds into the dough while rolling.
8. Cover and allow to it rise or proof for 15-20 minutes.
9. Roll into small circles, about ⅛- to ¼-inch thick. Cover with a towel.
10. Heat up a tawa or flat pan.
11. Without the traditional tandoori oven, you can cook the naan over the stovetop in two ways:
12. First method
13. Place a circle of dough on the tawa. When in begins to bubble, flip it over.
14. When the other side is cooked, pick up the naan with a pair of tongs and hold it directly over the flame (set the tawa aside for a while). Flip over when the naan puffs up. The naan should have brown spots all over.
15. Spread with some butter or ghee. Serve immediately or place in a casserole dish to keep warm and moist before serving.
16. Second method (for this, do not use a nonstick tawa)
17. Moisten the top of a circle of dough with about a teaspoon or two of water. This will make it stick to the tawa, so you can turn the pan without having the bread fall off.
18. Place the naan circle wet side down, on the tawa.
19. When the top or visible side begins to darken slightly, that means the other side is cooked.
20. Hold the handle of the tawa and flip the whole pan over so that the top side of the naan is directly over the flame. Position the pan in such a way that the naan can be reached by the flame and, at the same time, you can still see it cooking (pan should be slightly slanted over the flame). When the side exposed to the flame begins to bubble and is covered with brown spots, the naan is cooked.
21. Spread with some butter or ghee. Serve immediately or place in a casserole to keep warm and moist before serving.

LAMB VINDALOO

Serves: 8 - **Preparation Time:** 15 minutes - **Cooking time:** 1 hour 45 minutes

INGREDIENTS

For spice paste:

- 6 tablespoons grainy mustard
- 4 teaspoons ground cumin
- 4 teaspoons turmeric powder
- 1 ½ teaspoons cayenne pepper, or according to taste
- 2 tablespoons red wine vinegar

For lamb:

- 4 pounds boneless lamb shoulder, cut into 1 ½–inch cubes
- 4 tablespoons mustard or vegetable oil, divided
- Salt and pepper
- 1 large sweet onion, diced
- 12 cloves garlic, minced
- 3 cups coconut milk
- 1 cup water

For garnish:

- Fresh cilantro, chopped

DIRECTIONS

1. Combine the spice paste ingredients and set it aside to allow the flavors to meld.
2. Rub lamb chunks with 2 tablespoons of oil. Season with salt and pepper.
3. Heat a large pot to medium-high heat and sear the lamb cubes in batches, until well-browned. Remove from pot and set aside.
4. Add the remaining oil to the same pot.
5. Cook the onion until tender (about 5 minutes).
6. Add the garlic and sauté until fragrant (about 1 minute).
7. Add the spice paste and sauté for another minute.
8. Pour in the coconut milk and water, and return the lamb to the pot. Add more water, if needed, to cover the lamb.
9. Bring it to a simmer and reduce the heat to medium-low.
10. Continue simmering until the meat is tender (about 1 ½ hours).
11. Garnish with cilantro and serve with rice.

CLASSIC LAMB CURRY

Serves: 4 - **Preparation Time:** 15 minutes plus optional 1 hour marinating time - **Cooking time:** 1 hour 20 minutes

INGREDIENTS

- 3 tablespoons mustard or vegetable oil
- 1 onion, finely chopped
- 4 cloves garlic, crushed
- ½ teaspoon cumin seeds
- 1 pound lamb stew meat, cubed
- Water to cover the lamb, as needed
- 1 large potato, peeled and cubed

For marinade:

- 3 tablespoons tomato paste
- 2 teaspoons ground coriander
- Salt, to taste
- 2 teaspoons garam masala
- 1 ½ teaspoons turmeric powder
- 1 teaspoon red chili powder, or according to taste

DIRECTIONS

1. Combine the ingredients for the marinade, and toss in the lamb cubes. Let marinate in refrigerator for 1 hour.
2. Heat the oil in a saucepan or pot. Add the cumin seeds and allow them to sizzle (about 30 seconds).
3. Add the onion and garlic and sauté until fragrant and onion is tender (about 10 minutes).
4. Add the marinated lamb as well as the marinade. Add about ½ cup water, or as needed, and stir. Bring it to a simmer, and cook until the lamb is tender (about 1 hour).
5. Add the potato cubes and cook until the potatoes are tender (about 10 minutes).
6. Serve with rice or naan.

LAMB IN CREAMY & SPICY SAUCE (LAMB MASALA)

Serves: 6 - **Preparation Time:** 5 minutes - **Cooking time:** 1 hour 40 minutes

INGREDIENTS

- 1 tablespoon ghee
- 1 onion, coarsely chopped
- 4 cloves garlic, crushed
- 1 tablespoon ginger, grated
- 1 long green chili, seeded, finely chopped

- 2 teaspoons coriander powder
- 2 teaspoons cumin powder
- 1 ¾ pounds lamb rump steaks, cut into 1-inch pieces
- 1 ½ cups yogurt
- 2 ripe tomatoes, finely chopped
- 2 tablespoons tomato paste
- 2 teaspoons garam masala, or according to taste
- 2 tablespoons tamarind puree
- Salt and pepper
- Fresh cilantro leaves, chopper, for garnish

DIRECTIONS

1. Heat the ghee in a saucepan over medium heat.
2. Sauté the onion, garlic, ginger, and chili until the onion is tender (about 5 minutes).
3. Add the coriander and cumin powders and cook 1 minute longer or until fragrant.
4. Add the lamb and stir.
5. When the lamb cubes are slightly browned, stir in the yogurt, tomatoes, and tomato paste.
6. Reduce the heat. Cover and simmer, stirring occasionally, until the lamb is tender (about 1 ½ hours).
7. Add the garam masala, tamarind puree, salt, and pepper. Stir.
8. Cook a little longer to thicken the sauce, if needed.
9. Serve garnished with chopped cilantro.

FESTIVE LAMB IN CREAMY SAUCE (LAMB KORMA)

Serves: 4 - **Preparation Time:** 15 minutes plus 1 hour marinating time - **Cooking time:** 1 hour 20 minutes

INGREDIENTS

- 2 pounds lamb leg meat, in 1 ¼-inch cubes

For spice paste marinade:

- 1 medium onion, chopped
- 2 teaspoons ginger, grated
- 4 cloves garlic, minced
- 2 teaspoons coriander powder
- 2 teaspoons cumin powder
- 1 teaspoon cardamom seeds
- ¼ teaspoon cloves

- ¼ teaspoon ground cinnamon
- 3 long green chilies, seeded and chopped

For sauce:

- 2 tablespoons ghee
- 1 medium onion, sliced
- 2 ½ tablespoons tomato paste
- ½ cup plain yogurt
- ½ cup coconut cream
- ½ cup ground almonds
- ½ teaspoon sugar
- Salt and pepper, to taste
- Toasted almonds, slivered, for garnish

DIRECTIONS

1. Combine all the ingredients for the spice paste marinade in a food processor or spice grinder to make a paste. You may also use a mortar and pestle and pound the ingredients until smooth.
2. Rub the paste evenly over the lamb cubes. Refrigerate and let them marinate for 1 hour.
3. In a pot or saucepan, heat the ghee over low heat.
4. Add the sliced onion and cook for 5-7 minutes or until tender.
5. Adjust the heat to medium-high. Add the lamb in the spice paste and cook, stirring constantly, until the lamb is no longer pink (about 8-10 minutes).
6. Add the tomato paste, yogurt, coconut cream, ground almonds, and sugar.
7. Reduce the heat. Cover and simmer, stirring occasionally, until the lamb is tender (about 1 hour). Add a little water if the mixture dries out.
8. Season with salt and pepper.
9. Garnish with slivered almonds and serve.

CHICKEN TIKKA MASALA

Serves: 3-4 - **Preparation Time:** 5 minutes plus 20 minutes marinating time - **Cooking time:** 45-50 minutes

INGREDIENTS

- 1 pound boneless skinless chicken, cut into 1-inch cubes

For marinade:

- 2 ½ tablespoons yogurt
- 1 teaspoon freshly squeezed lemon juice
- ½ teaspoon turmeric powder

- ¼ teaspoon cayenne pepper or red chili powder, or according to taste
- ¼ teaspoon garam masala, or according to taste
- Salt and pepper, to taste

For sauce:

- 1 tablespoon mustard or vegetable oil
- 1 tablespoon butter
- 1 1-inch stick of cinnamon
- 1 large onion, chopped
- Salt, to taste
- 1 tablespoon ginger, grated
- 1 tablespoon garlic, crushed
- 1 tablespoon ground cumin
- ½ tablespoon ground coriander
- ½ tablespoon fenugreek leaves
- ¼ teaspoon cayenne pepper, or according to taste
- ¾ cup tomatoes, diced
- 2 tablespoons tomato paste
- 1 cup water

¾ teaspoon garam masala

- 1 tablespoon brown sugar
- ½ cup water, or as needed
- 4 tablespoons heavy cream

For garnish:

- Cilantro leaves, chopped

DIRECTIONS

1. Combine the marinade ingredients, and stir the chicken in. Cover and leave to marinate for about 20 minutes while you prepare other ingredients.
2. Heat the oil in a large pot over medium heat.
3. Add the cinnamon, onion, and salt. Cook for about 3-5 minutes or until the onions are slightly caramelized.
4. Add the ginger and garlic and cook for 1 minute or until fragrant.
5. Add the cumin, coriander, fenugreek, cayenne, tomatoes and tomato paste.
6. Cook, with occasional stirring. The mixture will thicken and the oil will separate from the spices. You will see the oil floating on the surface.
7. At this point, add the chicken to the same pot and cook for about 10 minutes.
8. Add the garam masala, brown sugar, and enough water to cover the chicken.

9. Reduce the heat to medium-low. Cover and simmer for 20-25 minutes. The chicken should be tender and the sauce should have thickened. The ideal consistency of the sauce should be like that of pasta sauce. Turn up the heat to thicken or add water to thin it.

10. Reduce the heat to low and add cream. Stir.

11. You may adjust the taste with seasonings, sugar, garam masala, and cayenne powder according to your taste.

12. Remove the cinnamon stick.

13. Serve garnished with chopped cilantro. Best with basmati rice or naan.

TANDOORI CHICKEN - STOVETOP METHOD

Serves: 4-6 - **Preparation Time:** 25 minutes plus 4 hours 20 minutes marinating time - **Cooking time:** 40-45 minutes

INGREDIENTS

- 1 ½ pounds chicken breasts or thighs

For the first marinade:

- 2 teaspoons minced ginger
- 2 teaspoons minced garlic
- 2 teaspoons paprika
- 2 teaspoons ground coriander
- Juice of half a lemon or of 1 lime
- Salt and fresh black pepper

For the second marinade:

- ⅓ cup yogurt
- 1 tablespoon ginger, grated
- 3 cloves garlic, minced
- 1 teaspoon coriander powder
- 1 teaspoon cumin powder

1 teaspoon garam masala

- ¼ teaspoon turmeric powder
- 1 teaspoon black pepper
- 1 tablespoon salt, or to taste
- 1 teaspoon red chili powder (preferably Kashmiri), or according to taste
- 1 teaspoon fenugreek leaves
- 2 drops red food color (optional)

- 1 tablespoon mustard or vegetable oil

For baking:

- 1 small onion, cut into wedges
- 2 small carrots, diced
- ½ bell pepper, diced
- 1 tablespoon mustard or vegetable oil

For stove-top grilling and smoking (optional):

- 1 tablespoon juice of lime or lemon
- 1-2 teaspoons chaat masala , or according to taste
- 1 small piece charcoal
- ½ teaspoon vegetable oil

For garnish:

- Cilantro, chopped

DIRECTIONS

1. Wash the chicken with warm salted water. Drain well and pat it dry with paper towels. You may or may not want to remove the skin.
2. Make deep cuts into the chicken flesh for better absorption of the marinade.
3. Combine the ingredients for the first marinade. Rub it into the chicken, making sure to rub into the cuts in the flesh. Spread it as evenly as possible. Cover, and allow it to marinate for 15- 20 minutes.
4. In another bowl, combine all the ingredients for the second marinade, EXCEPT the oil. Immerse the chicken into this marinade and rub it evenly and thoroughly all over the chicken. Drizzle 1 tablespoon of oil over the chicken. Cover and marinate for at least 4 hours, or overnight.
5. When the chicken is ready, preheat the oven to 425°F.
6. Line a baking tray or shallow baking pan with foil. Place the vegetables in a layer close to the center of the tray to make a "bed" for the chicken.
7. Put the chicken pieces on top of the vegetables. Spread any leftover marinade over the chicken. Drizzle with oil.
8. Bake for 15 minutes.
9. Reduce the temperature of the oven to 400°F. Bake for 20-25 minutes more.

To get a grilled and smoked effect, this step is optional but it will enhance the flavor.

10. Heat a nonstick pan over medium-high heat.
11. Place the baked chicken in the pan and brown it for 1 minute per side. Remove the pan from heat.
12. Hold the piece of charcoal with a pair of tongs and touch the coal to the flame.
13. Place the heated charcoal in a piece of aluminum foil. Place this in the middle of the pan containing the chicken. Pour oil over the charcoal to release smoke. Cover the pan and let it smoke for 1-3 minutes.
14. Garnish the chicken with chopped cilantro and serve with baked vegetables, sliced sweet onions, and

lime wedges. Best with rice and raita .

CHICKEN BIRYANI

Serves: 4-6 - **Preparation Time:** 20 minutes plus 1 hour soaking time - **Cooking time:** 45 minutes

INGREDIENTS:

- 1 ½ pounds chicken pieces (may be boneless or bone-in)

For rice:

- 2 cups Basmati rice, uncooked
- 4 cups water for soaking rice
- 6-8 cups water to boil rice
- 2 tablespoons vegetable oil
- 3 pieces bay leaf
- 1 tablespoon salt

For marinade:

- 3 tablespoons curry powder
- ½-1 teaspoon red chili powder, or according to taste
- 1 tablespoon ginger garlic paste
- ¼ teaspoon salt
- ¼ teaspoon ground cinnamon
- ¼ teaspoon turmeric powder
- ⅓ cup yogurt
- 2 tablespoons coriander leaves, chopped
- 1 tablespoon mint leaves, chopped
- 2 teaspoons freshly squeezed lime juice
- ¼ cup vegetable oil

For vegetables:

- 1 tablespoon vegetable oil
- 2 small onions, cut into rings
- 2 pieces green chili, halved
- Pinch of salt, or as needed
- 1 chicken bouillon cube, crumbled (optional)
- For final layering:
- 3 tablespoons cilantro leaves
- 2 tablespoons mint leaves
- 2 tablespoons raisins

- 1 ½ teaspoons saffron threads, soaked in 2 teaspoons hot rice broth
- 1 tablespoon ghee

For garnish:

- 1 tablespoon green onions, chopped
- 1 tablespoon sliced almonds

DIRECTIONS:

1. Put the rice in a medium bowl and cover it with water. Soak for 1 hour.
2. Wash the chicken, drain it well, and wipe it dry.
3. In a large bowl, combine all marinade ingredients and rub it thoroughly into the chicken pieces. Cover with cling wrap and marinate for 20 minutes in the refrigerator.
4. Drain the soaked rice. The grains should have lengthened noticeably.
5. Bring about 6-8 cups of water in a medium pot to a rolling boil.
6. Add the oil, bay leaves, and salt.
7. Add the drained rice to the boiling water. The amount of water should be enough to make the rice grains "dance" in the bubbling water.
8. Cook until the rice is about 60-70% cooked (about 3 minutes). The grains should break into pieces when pinched. In the mouth, the grain will feel cooked outside but uncooked inside. It is better to stop cooking while the grains are half cooked than to overcook. Strain the rice out of the water, saving 2 teaspoons of the hot broth.
9. In a small cup, mix the 2 teaspoons of hot broth from the rice with the saffron threads. Let them soak.
10. Meanwhile, prepare the chicken sauce. Heat a large, heavy-bottomed or nonstick pot over medium-high heat. NOTE: The pot should have a tight-fitting lid.
11. Add the oil and fry onions until golden brown (about 7-10 minutes).
12. Scoop out half of the onions and set them aside.
13. Add the green chilies and salt to remaining onions in the pot. Stir until fragrant.
14. Add the chicken and marinade and mix well. Mix in the chicken bouillon cube (optional). Cover and cook for 10 minutes.
15. Arrange the chicken pieces so they are all touching the bottom of pot. This is the first layer.
16. Spread half the rice over the chicken, as evenly as possible. This is the second layer.
17. Spread the cilantro and mint leaves over the rice layer. Sprinkle with some of the fried onion.
18. Add the remaining rice to form another layer.
19. Sprinkle with remaining fried onion rings and add the raisins. Pour the liquid with the saffron in a circular motion over the rice, and repeat with the ghee.
20. Reduce the heat to low. Cover and cook for 20 minutes.
21. Turn off the heat, but do not remove the lid. Let it stand for 5-10 more minutes before removing lid.
22. Open and dig into pot to get the chicken pieces. Do not mix. Simply spoon some rice onto serving dish with the chicken.

23. Garnish with cilantro and almond slices.

QUICK CHICKEN CURRY

Serves: 4-6 **- Preparation Time:** 5 minutes **- Cooking time:** 15-20 minutes

INGREDIENTS

- 2-3 pounds cooked chicken, poached or roasted
- 1 ½ tablespoons mustard or vegetable oil
- 1 small onion, thinly sliced
- 1 teaspoon ginger, grated
- 3 cloves garlic, minced
- 1 tablespoon curry powder
- ½-1 teaspoon red chili flakes
- 1 medium tomato, diced
- ½ cup yogurt
- 1 (14-ounce) can coconut milk
- 1-2 pieces bay leaf
- ½ teaspoon salt, or to taste
- ¼ teaspoon black pepper
- ½ teaspoon sugar (optional)
- ¼ cup fresh cilantro leaves, roughly chopped
- 1 cup white rice

DIRECTIONS

1. Shred the pre-cooked chicken, or cut it into bite-sized pieces.
2. Heat the oil in a frying pan or wok over medium-high heat and sauté the onions and ginger until fragrant and the onion is tender (about 5-8 minutes).
3. Add garlic and sauté about a minute longer until fragrant.
4. Add the chicken and stir-fry. For roast chicken pieces, heat through. If you're using poached chicken, cook until slightly browned.
5. Add the curry powder, chili flakes and tomato. Stir-fry for about 3 minutes, or until the tomatoes are slightly mushy.
6. Reduce the heat to medium-low and add yogurt, coconut milk, bay leaves, black pepper, salt, and sugar (optional). Stir and simmer until thickened, about 3-5 minutes.
7. Adjust the seasoning and spices, if desired.
8. Remove from the heat, sprinkle with cilantro, and serve with rice or naan.

CHICKEN MADRAS

Serves: 4 - **Preparation Time:** 30 minutes - **Cooking time:** 30 minutes to 1 hour

INGREDIENTS

- 4 boneless skinless chicken breasts or thighs, cut into bite-sized pieces

For marinade:

- 1 ½ tablespoons freshly squeezed lemon juice
- 1 teaspoon garam masala
- Salt, to taste

For sauce:

- 2 tablespoons ghee or vegetable oil
- 1 large onion, finely chopped
- 3-5 tablespoons Madras curry paste
- 1 (16-ounce) can chopped tomatoes
- ½ cup desiccated coconut

For garnish:

- ¼ cup fresh cilantro, chopped

DIRECTIONS

1. Combine the ingredients for the marinade and toss in the chicken pieces. Set aside.
2. Heat the oil in a karahi/wok, or frying pan. Sauté the onion until it is almost golden in color (5-8 minutes).
3. Add the chicken and cook for 5 minutes, stirring constantly.
4. Add the Madras paste and stir to distribute the flavor, than cook for 2 more minutes.
5. Add the tomato and coconut, cover, and let it simmer for 20 minutes. The chicken should be cooked through.
6. Add more salt or madras paste, if desired.
7. Garnish with cilantro and serve with rice or naan.

BUTTER CHICKEN (MURGH MAKHAN)

Serves: 6 - **Preparation Time:** 15 minutes - **Cooking time:** 45 minutes

INGREDIENTS

- 1 cup butter, divided
- 1 onion, minced
- 1 tablespoon minced garlic
- 1 ½ pounds boneless skinless chicken breast, cut into bite-sized chunks

- 2 tablespoons vegetable oil
- 2 tablespoons tandoori masala
- 1 (15-ounce) can tomato sauce
- 3 cups heavy cream
- 2 teaspoons salt
- 1 teaspoon cayenne pepper
- 1 teaspoon garam masala

DIRECTIONS

1. Preheat the oven to 375°F.
2. Take about 2 tablespoons of the butter and melt it in a karahi (or any skillet) over medium heat.
3. Add the onion and garlic and cook for 15 minutes, stirring occasionally, or until the onion becomes dark brown in color.
4. In a bowl, combine the chicken with the oil and toss to coat. Add the tandoori masala and mix well.
5. Arrange the chicken pieces in one layer on a baking sheet.
6. Bake for about 12 minutes, or until the chicken is thoroughly cooked.
7. In another pan, melt the rest of the butter over medium-high heat.
8. Stir in the tomato sauce, cream, salt, cayenne, and garam masala.
9. Reduce the heat to medium low and simmer for 30 minutes.
10. Add the caramelized onion and the baked chicken, and simmer for 5 minutes.

GOAN FISH CURRY

Serves: 4-6 - Preparation Time: 15 minutes **- Cooking time:** 20-30 minutes

INGREDIENTS

- 2 tablespoons vegetable oil
- 1 large onion, finely chopped
- 4 large cloves fresh garlic, minced
- 1 cup water
- 1 teaspoon salt, or to taste
- 1 cup coconut milk
- 2-3 tablespoons tamarind paste
- 1 ½ pounds fish fillets, 1 inch thick, cut into 2-inch pieces
- ¼ cup finely chopped fresh cilantro, including soft stems

For spice mix:

- 3 dried red chili peppers, broken into pieces
- 1 teaspoon coriander seeds

- 1 teaspoon cumin seeds
- ¼ teaspoon ground turmeric

DIRECTIONS

1. Grind together the red chili peppers, coriander, cumin, and turmeric in a small spice grinder. Set aside.
2. Heat the oil in a large nonstick wok or saucepan over medium-high heat and stir-fry the onion for 5 minutes or until golden.
3. Add the garlic and stir 1 minute, then stir in the spice mixture and cook 2 minutes more.
4. Pour in the water and coconut milk. Bring to a boil, stirring constantly. Reduce the heat and simmer for 5 minutes.
5. add the tamarind paste and salt. stir well.
6. add the fish and continue simmering for 10-15 minutes, or until the fish is opaque and easy to flake with a fork.
7. sprinkle with cilantro and serve.

FISH SKEWERS (FISH TANDOORI TIKKA)

Serves: 4 - Preparation Time: 10 minutes plus 8 hours and 10 minutes marinating time **- Cooking time:** 15 minutes

INGREDIENTS

- 1 ½ pounds fish fillets, cut into 1 ½-inch cubes

For first marinade:

- Salt, to taste
- ⅛ teaspoon red chili powder
- 4 tablespoons freshly squeezed lemon juice

For second marinade:

- 1 cup yogurt
- ½ teaspoon garam masala
- ¼ teaspoon red chili powder
- ¼ teaspoon cumin powder
- ¼ teaspoon pepper powder
- 2 cloves garlic, minced
- 1 teaspoon ginger, minced

For garnish:

- Pinch of chaat masala
- Lemon wedges

DIRECTIONS

1. Wipe the fish with paper towels to dry.
2. Gently rub the ingredients for the first marinade all over the fish. Cover, and refrigerate for 10 minutes.
3. In a bowl, combine ingredients for second marinade.
4. Gently massage the mixture onto the fish and let it marinate for 6-8 hours.
5. Skewer the fish pieces and grill for about 7-8 minutes on each side.
6. sprinkle with chaat masala and serve with wedges of lemon.

MIXED SEAFOOD CURRY

Serves: 6 - **Preparation Time:** 20 minutes - **Cooking time:** 15 minutes

INGREDIENTS

- 2 tablespoons vegetable oil
- 1 medium onion, halved and sliced
- 1 tablespoon ginger, minced
- 1 tablespoon garlic, minced
- 2-3 pieces green chili
- ½ teaspoon red chili powder (optional)
- ½ teaspoon turmeric powder
- 1 (14-ounce) can light coconut milk
- 3 tablespoons lime juice
- 1 tablespoons curry powder, or according to taste
- 1 tablespoon brown sugar
- 12 medium shrimp, peeled (tails left on) and deveined
- 12 sea scallops, halved
- 2 tablespoons chopped cilantro
- Salt to taste

DIRECTIONS

1. Heat oil in a karahi/kadai or wok over medium-high heat.
2. Sauté the onion until tender, about 2-3 minutes.
3. Stir in the ginger, garlic, and green chili, and sauté until fragrant, about 1 minute.
4. Add red chili powder (optional), turmeric, coconut milk, lime juice, curry powder, and brown sugar. Bring to a simmer and cook for 5 minutes.
5. Add the shrimp, scallops, cilantro, and salt, and cook until the shrimps and scallops become opaque, about 5 minutes.
6. adjust the flavor with more salt and spices if needed.

FISH BIRYANI

Serves: 4-6 - **Preparation Time:** 10-15 minutes, plus 1 hour soaking - **Cooking time:** 30-35 minutes

INGREDIENTS

For rice:

- 2 cups basmati rice, presoaked for 1 hour and drained
- 2 tablespoons olive oil, for rice
- 3 cups water

For sautéing:

- ¼ cup vegetable oil
- 1 medium red onion, sliced
- 1 medium yellow onion, sliced
- 1 tablespoon salt
- 1 tablespoon black pepper
- 1 tablespoon red chili powder
- 1 tablespoon garam masala
- 1 tablespoon coriander powder
- 1 tablespoon turmeric powder
- 1 tablespoon cumin seeds
- 1 tablespoon minced garlic
- 1 tablespoon ginger paste
- 2 pounds fish nuggets or fillets cut in medium-size pieces, deep fried

For layering:

- ½ cup olive oil
- 3-4 drops red-orange food color, dissolved in 1 tablespoon water (optional)
- 3 tablespoons cashews
- 3 tablespoons almonds (optional)
- 3-6 green and red chilies, halved
- Cilantro, chopped

DIRECTIONS

1. Place the basmati rice in a saucepan and add the olive oil. Mix well. Pour in the water and turn the heat to medium high. Cover and let it cook until it starts to steam and the rice is half-cooked but beginning to dry out. Turn off the heat, and leave it covered to sit.
2. Meanwhile, heat the oil for sautéing in another skillet or karahi/kadai.
3. Sauté the onions until browned. Separate half of the onions to be used later.
4. Push the onions in the pan to the side, and sauté the ginger and garlic until fragrant. Mix them in with

the onions.

5. Add the rest of the spices and mix well.
6. add fried fish nuggets/pieces, stir and cook to heat through.
7. cover and simmer for 2 minutes, for the fish to absorb the flavors.
8. Get a deep, heavy-bottomed pan. Coat it thinly with olive oil and heat to medium-high.
9. Spread half of the partly cooked rice and sprinkle with some onion slices.
10. Spread about half of the chilies, nuts, parsley, and cilantro over the rice layer.
11. Add half of the food color, pouring over the contents of the pot.
12. Arrange half of the fish nuggets or pieces on top.
13. Repeat the layering with rice, onions, chilies, nuts, parsley, cilantro, food color and fish.
14. Reduce the heat to low.
15. Cover with aluminum foil, seal sides, and replace the lid.
16. Cook 10 minutes. You may place the pot over a tawa or a skillet to prevent scorching at the bottom.
17. Remove the lid and mix a little to distribute the flavors and colors.
18. Spoon onto serving plate or tray.

MALABAR TILAPIA

Serves: 3-4 - **Preparation Time:** 15 minutes plus 5-10 minutes soaking time - **Cooking time:** 40 minutes
INGREDIENTS

For marinade:

- 2 pounds fish fillets, cut into medium pieces
- 1 teaspoon red chili powder
- ¼ teaspoon turmeric powder
- Salt, to taste

For tamarind juice:

- 1 tablespoon tamarind puree
- ⅔ cup hot water

For gravy:

- 2 tablespoons coconut oil
- 1 medium onion, sliced
- 15 curry leaves (methi neem), divided
- 1 tablespoon coriander powder
- 2 tablespoons fish masala (meen masala) powder
- 1 medium onion, quartered
- 2 plum tomatoes, quartered

- 1 cup grated coconut
- 1 cup water

DIRECTIONS

1. Wash the fish. Drain it, and wipe dry with paper towels.
2. Mix the ingredients for the marinade together, and coat the fish with it. Set aside.
3. Soak the tamarind in hot water for about 5-10 minutes. Squeeze and strain out pulp or any solids. Set aside.
4. Heat the coconut oil in a pan or karahi and sauté the sliced onions and curry leaves for about 3-5 minutes or until the onion has browned. Remove from the pan and set aside.
5. Using remaining oil, sauté the coriander and fish masala until fragrant.
6. In a blender or food processor, combine the quartered onion, tomatoes, grated coconut and the sautéed spices. Blend until smooth. You may add a few teaspoons of water from the measured amount if it is too dry. Pour in the rest of the water and the tamarind juice. Pulse to mix.
7. Pour the blended mixture back into the same pan. Stir, and bring it to a boil.
8. Reduce the heat to medium low. Cover and simmer for 15 minutes, with occasional stirring.
9. Add the marinated fish and simmer for 15 minutes or until fish is cooked.
10. Taste and adjust flavors with salt and more spices, if needed.
11. Add the browned onion and curry leaves and cover. Turn off the heat.
12. Serve with rice.

TAMARIND SCALLOPS (AMBLI WARA)

Serves: 4 - **Preparation Time:** 10 minutes - **Cooking time:** 4-8 minutes

INGREDIENTS

- 2 large cloves garlic, chopped
- ¾ teaspoon salt
- 2 teaspoons tamarind paste
- 2 ½ teaspoons sugar
- ½ teaspoon chili powder
- 2 tablespoons vegetable oil
- 12 large scallops
- 1-2 tablespoons butter, unsalted
- 1 lemon, cut into wedges

DIRECTIONS

1. Make a paste of the garlic and salt by pounding them together in a mortar and pestle.
2. Add the tamarind paste, sugar, chili powder, and vegetable oil to the garlic paste, and mix well.

3. Toss scallops in this marinade, making sure to coat each evenly. Let sit for up to 5 minutes.

4. Heat a frying pan or karahi over medium-high heat, and melt the butter.

5. Arrange the scallops in the butter and let them brown on one side, about 2-4 minutes.

6. Flip them over to brown on the other side.

7. Serve with lemon wedges.

CLASSIC CHEESE SKEWERS (PANEER TIKKA)

Serves: 3-4 - **Preparation Time:** 1 hour - **Cooking time:** 20 minutes

INGREDIENTS

- 2-3 tablespoons oil

For skewers:

- 10 ounces Indian cottage cheese (paneer), cut into ¼-inch by 1 ½-inch cubes
- 1 small green bell pepper, cut into 1-inch squares
- 1 small red or yellow bell pepper (optional), cut into 1-inch squares
- 1 medium tomato, cut into squares and seeded
- 1 medium onion, peeled and halved, layers separated

For the marinade:

- 2 ¼ cups thick yogurt or hung curds (dahi)
- 4 tablespoons gram flour (besan)
- ½ teaspoon turmeric powder
- ½ teaspoon black pepper powder or white pepper powder/kali mirch powder
- ½ teaspoon carom seeds
- ½ teaspoon caraway seeds (shahjeera)
- ½ teaspoon dry fenugreek leaves, crushed
- 1 teaspoon coriander powder
- 1 teaspoon cumin powder
- 1 teaspoon chaat masala powder
- 1 teaspoon garam masala powder or tandoori masala powder
- 1 teaspoon dry mango powder (amchur)
- 2 teaspoons kashmiri red chili powder or 1 teaspoon red chili powder
- ¾ tablespoon ginger-garlic paste
- 5 cloves garlic, crushed
- ¾ teaspoon ginger, crushed

- ¾ teaspoon lime juice
- ¾ teaspoon salt, or to taste

For garnish:

- Chaat masala
- Lemon wedges

DIRECTIONS

1. Whisk the ingredients for the marinade thoroughly. Taste and adjust according to your preference.
2. Drop in the cheese and vegetables and mix with your hands.
3. Cover and refrigerate. Let marinate for 45 minutes to overnight.
4. Heat a tawa or nonstick frying pan over low or medium flame and add the oil.
5. Separate paneer from veggies, as they fry faster.
6. Coat with marinade and fry until browned on one side. Flip over to fry other side.
7. Drain on paper towels, and repeat with the vegetables.
8. After frying, skewer the fried cheese and veggies on wooden skewers or toothpicks.
9. Sprinkle with chaat masala and serve with lemon wedges. Goes well with mint chutney and pickles.

CREAMY SPINACH & FENUGREEK WITH INDIAN CHEESE (SAAG PANEER)

Serves: 4 - **Preparation Time:** 20 minutes - **Cooking time:** 20 minutes

INGREDIENTS

- 2-3 tablespoons butter, ghee or coconut oil
- 10 ounces paneer , cubed
- 1 1-inch piece of cinnamon stick
- 2 dried red chilies, broken into pieces
- 1 small bay leaf
- 1 medium tomato, chopped
- ½ teaspoon red chili powder (lal mirch)
- ¼ teaspoon turmeric powder
- 1 ⅓ tablespoons gram (besan) or corn flour (makki ka atta)
- Salt, to taste
- ½ cup water
- 1 teaspoon dried fenugreek leaves, crushed

For spinach paste:

- 1 bunch spinach (palak)
- 1 cup fenugreek (methi) leaves

- 2-3 tablespoons daikon (mooli), peeled and chopped

For garlic paste:

- 2 dry red chilies
- 1 medium sized onion, chopped
- 1 green chili, chopped
- 1 teaspoon fresh ginger, minced
- 3 cloves garlic, minced

DIRECTIONS

1. To make spinach paste: Sprinkle the fenugreek leaves with salt. Let it sit for 10-20 minutes, and then squeeze to remove the juice and reduce the bitterness. Rinse well and drain. Immerse in boiling water for 5 minutes, together with the spinach and daikon. Drain well and wipe off excess water. Put in a blender and blend to a coarse paste.
2. To make garlic paste: Combine the ingredients for garlic paste and blend until smooth.
3. Fry the paneer cubes until light golden brown. Set aside.
4. Add more oil or butter to the pan, if needed, and stir-fry the cinnamon, red chilies and bay leaves until fragrant.
5. Add the garlic paste and stir-fry until browned.
6. Add the tomatoes, red chili powder, and turmeric, and continue cooking until the tomatoes have softened.

    Add the spinach paste, and mix in the gram or corn flour. Stir to remove lumps.
7. Add the salt and water. Simmer for 5-7 minutes.
8. Add the fried paneer cubes and heat through.
9. Crush the dried fenugreek in your hand as you add it to the mix, and simmer for 1 minute.
10. Serve while hot with bread, such as naan.

LENTILS IN TEMPERED GHEE & SPICES (DAL TADKA)

Serves: 4 to 5 - **Preparation Time:** 10 minutes plus presoaking for 1-2 hours - **Cooking time:** 55 minutes to 1 hour

INGREDIENTS

For dal:

- ½ cup split pigeon pea lentils, soaked for 1-2 hours, rinsed and drained
- ½ cup split pink lentils, soaked for 1-2 hours, rinsed and drained
- 1 medium onion, chopped
- 2 medium tomatoes, chopped

- 1 green chili, chopped
- 1 teaspoon ginger, grated
- 1 teaspoon turmeric powder
- A pinch of asafetida
- 2 tablespoons cream
- ¼ teaspoon garam masala powder
- 1 teaspoon dry fenugreek leaves, crushed
- 1 tablespoon cilantro leaves, chopped
- Salt, to taste

For the tempering:
- 1 ½ tablespoons ghee or butter
- 1 teaspoon cumin seeds
- 2-3 red chilies
- ⅛ teaspoon asafetida
- 5 cloves garlic, finely chopped
- ½ teaspoon red chili powder

For garnish:
- 1 tablespoon cilantro leaves, chopped

For smoky flavor (dhunga r method):
- Small piece of natural charcoal
- ¼ teaspoon ghee or oil

DIRECTIONS

1. Place the re-soaked lentils in a deep pot and add 4-5 cups water. Add the chopped onions, tomato, green chilies, and ginger.
2. Bring it to a boil. Remove the lid or cover only slightly and simmer for about 45 minutes, or until the lentils are soft and creamy. You may need to add more water while cooking to prevent them from drying out and scorching.
3. Add the turmeric powder and asafetida. Stir well.
4. Add the cream, garam masala powder, crushed dried fenugreek leaves, chopped cilantro leaves, and salt. Remove from heat.
5. Mix well and taste. Adjust the salt if needed.
6. For smoky flavor (dhungar method): using a pair of tongs, heat up a small piece of charcoal until it becomes red hot. Place the red hot charcoal in a small steel bowl. Pour about ¼ teaspoon of oil or ghee on the charcoal. The charcoal will start to emit smoke. Place this bowl on the dal. Cover the pot for 1 to 2 minutes. Remove the little bowl carefully with tongs. Cover the dal and set aside.
7. Tempering/tadka: heat the ghee or butter in a small pan over a low heat. Add the cumin seeds and mix

until they begin to crackle. Be careful not to burn them.

8. Add the red chilies, asafetida, and chopped garlic. Cook until the garlic is browned.

9. Add the red chili powder, stir, and switch off the heat. Pour the entire tempering, along with the butter or ghee, into the dal. You may or may not mix the tempering into the dal (some prefer it simply poured on top).

10. Garnish with cilantro leaves.

11. Serve hot with steamed basmati rice or Indian bread.

CUCUMBER, MINT & TOMATO SALAD (KACHUMBAR/KACHUMBER)

Serves: 2 - **Preparation Time:** 15 minutes - **Cooking time:** none

INGREDIENTS

- 1 large cucumber, peeled and finely chopped
- 4 plum tomatoes, finely chopped
- ½ sweet onion, very finely chopped
- 3-5 pieces green chili, seeded, very thinly sliced

For dressing:

- Salt, to taste
- ½ teaspoon sugar
- ¼ teaspoon cumin seeds, slightly crushed
- ¼ cup lemon juice
- 2 tablespoons fresh mint, finely chopped
- 1 tablespoon fresh cilantro, chopped

DIRECTIONS

1. Combine the ingredients for the dressing and let it sit to allow the flavors to meld. Adjust saltiness or sweetness according to taste.

2. Combine the prepared vegetables, chilies and onion.

3. Add to the dressing and refrigerate for 15 minutes.

4. Serve (best when chilled). Goes well with curries.

SPICY VEGETABLE STEW (VEGETABLE MASALA)

Serves: 4 - **Preparation Time:** 5 minutes - **Cooking time:** 40 minutes

INGREDIENTS

- 1 teaspoon fresh ginger, sliced
- 2 cloves garlic, peeled
- 1 (15-ounce) can diced tomatoes, undrained
- ½ teaspoon cayenne pepper
- 2 tablespoons canola or vegetable oil
- 1 medium onion, chopped
- 1 small bell pepper, diced
- 2 medium potatoes, peeled and cubed
- 1 carrot, sliced
- ½ cup peas
- 1 cup green beans
- 1 ½ teaspoon garam masala
- ½ teaspoon red chili powder
- 2 cups cauliflower florets
- ½ cup water
- ½ cup light coconut milk

DIRECTIONS

1. Use a mortar and pestle or food processor to chop the ginger and garlic.
2. Add the tomatoes and cayenne pepper, and pulse or stir to combine. Set aside.
3. Heat the oil in a saucepan or karahi over medium heat.
4. Sauté the onion and bell pepper until softened, about 10 minutes.
5. Add the potatoes, carrot, green beans, garam masala, and chili powder. Stir.
6. Cover, reduce heat, and simmer for 10 minutes.
7. Add the cauliflower, peas, tomato mixture, and water. Continue simmering for 20 more minutes.
8. Turn off the heat, add the coconut milk, and stir.
9. Serve immediately or let sit for stew to develop more heat and spiciness.

GREEN CHILI PICKLE (ACHAR OR MIRCHI-KA-ACHAR)

Serves: 4 - **Preparation Time:** 5-10 minutes, plus overnight drying time - **Cooking time:** none

INGREDIENTS

- 10-12 small hot chilies, washed and drained
- 1 cup fresh ginger, peeled and julienned

- 2 whole lemons
- ½ tablespoon salt
- ¼ tablespoon turmeric powder

DIRECTIONS

1. Wash and wipe the chilies dry. It's best to wash the day before and leave them to air dry overnight.
2. Wash a glass jar with a tight lid and dry thoroughly.
3. Cut the lemons in half and microwave for 10 seconds to soften the pulp.
4. Squeeze the lemon juice into a glass or glass bowl. Add the salt and turmeric to the juice. Mix well.
5. Stir in the chilies and ginger, and transfer the mixture to the prepared jar.
6. Seal the jar and keep it refrigerated. Shake the jar at least once a day.
7. The pickles can be served after 2 days but the flavor will be best by the third or fourth day.

MANGO CHUTNEY

Serves: 5 - **Preparation Time:** 10 minutes - **Cooking time:** 1 hour 10 minutes

INGREDIENTS

- 1 tablespoon cooking oil
- 2 teaspoons fresh ginger, finely minced
- 2 cloves garlic, finely minced
- 1 red chili, sliced
- 2 teaspoons whole nigella seeds
- 1 teaspoon ground coriander
- ½ teaspoon ground cumin
- ¼ teaspoon turmeric
- ¼ teaspoon ground cardamom
- ¼ teaspoon ground cloves
- ¼ teaspoon ground cinnamon
- 4-5 (about 2 pounds) ripe mangoes, peeled and diced
- 2 cups white granulated sugar
- ¼ teaspoon salt
- 1 cup white vinegar

DIRECTIONS

1. Heat the oil in a pot over medium-high heat.
2. Add ginger, garlic and red chili. Sauté for 1 minute.
3. Add all the other spices and sauté for another minute.
4. Next, add the mangoes, sugar, salt and vinegar. Stir, and bring to a boil.

5. Reduce the heat to medium-low and simmer for 1 hour.

6. Mash with a potato masher to break the mango into smaller pieces. Allow the mixture to cool before storing.

7. Place in jars.

8. Will keep for 2 months, in sealed jars, in the refrigerator.

9. May be consumed immediately, but it's best to keep it for 2 days before eating to get the best flavor.

HERBED YOGURT WITH CUCUMBER (RAITA)

Serves: 6 - **Preparation Time:** 15 minutes - **Cooking time:** none

INGREDIENTS

- ½ medium cucumber, washed and dried
- 1 cup plain yogurt
- ¼ teaspoon salt
- ¼ teaspoon cumin
- ¼ teaspoon coriander
- ¼ cup fresh cilantro, chopped
- ¼ cup mint leaves, chopped
- ½ teaspoon fresh ginger, peeled and grated

DIRECTIONS

1. Peel the cucumber and cut it lengthwise. Scoop out the seeds and julienne the flesh. Place in it a strainer to drain any excess moisture. Sprinkle with a dash of salt, and set aside.

2. Stir together the yogurt, salt, cumin, and coriander in a bowl.

3. Add cilantro, mint leaves and grated ginger. Mix well.

4. Press down on the julienned cucumber to squeeze out any moisture.

5. Add it to the yogurt mixture and stir.

6. Serve chilled. Great with indian bread and curries.

INDIAN-STYLE VEGETABLE STIR-FRY (JALFREZI)

Serves: 3-4 - **Preparation Time:** 15 minutes - **Cooking time:** 20 minutes

INGREDIENTS

- 1 ½ cups paneer, cubed

- 1-2 tablespoons vegetable oil
- ½ teaspoon cumin seeds
- ½ teaspoon nigella seeds (kalonji)
- 1 cup onion, thinly sliced
- 1 teaspoon ginger, freshly minced
- 1 teaspoon garlic, freshly minced
- ¾ teaspoon red chili, or according to taste
- 2 teaspoons coriander powder
- ¼ teaspoon turmeric powder
- 1 cup canned whole tomatoes, crushed
- ½ cup of carrots, julienned
- ½ cup green peas (optional)
- ½ cup cauliflower, sliced into bite-size pieces (optional)
- ½ cup baby corn, halved lengthwise
- 1 cup green pepper, julienned
- 1 cup water
- ½ cup ripe tomato, cubed
- 1 tablespoon ketchup
- ½ teaspoon dried fenugreek leaves

1 teaspoon garam masala

DIRECTIONS

1. Heat a pan with oil and fry the panee r on both sides until golden brown. Drain it on paper towels.
2. Use the remaining oil (add a little more, if needed) in the pan to fry the cumin and nigella. Allow it to crackle for about 30 seconds.
3. Add the onion and cook until translucent.
4. Add the ginger and garlic, and cook until fragrant, about 2 minutes.
5. Stir in the chili, coriander and turmeric powders. Reduce the heat, if necessary, so as not to burn the spices.
6. Stir in canned tomato, carrots, peas, cauliflower, baby corn and green pepper. Mix well.
7. Stir in the water and bring to a boil.
8. Cover and simmer for 3-5 minutes or until the carrots are tender.
9. Add the cubed tomato, ketchup, and fried paneer. Mix gently and simmer 4 minutes longer, or until the sauce has thickened to a gravy-like consistency.
10. Crush the fenugreek leaves in your hand as you sprinkle them into the pot. Stir in the garam masala and salt. Adjust the flavor with more salt or seasonings, if needed.
11. Remove from the heat and serve.

SPICY PANCAKES WITH POTATO FILLING (MASALA DOSA)

Serves: 5-6 **- Preparation Time:** 10 minutes plus 4-6 hours soaking time and 8 hours fermentation time - **Cooking time:** 40 minutes

INGREDIENTS

For the dosa batter:

- 2 cups short-grain rice
- ½ cup black gram or black lentil (urad dal)
- 1 teaspoon fenugreek seeds
- 4-5 cups cold water for soaking
- 1 cup cold water for grinding
- ½ teaspoon salt
- Vegetable oil, for frying

For potato filling:

- 3 tablespoons ghee or vegetable oil
- 1 teaspoon mustard seeds
- ½ teaspoon cumin seeds
- 2 small dried hot red peppers
- 1 medium onion, diced
- ½ teaspoon salt
- ½ teaspoon turmeric
- Pinch asafetida
- 1 tablespoon ginger, grated
- 6-8 curry leaves
- 4 cloves garlic, minced
- 2 small green chilies, finely chopped
- 1 ½ pounds yellow-fleshed potatoes, peeled and cubed
- ½ cup cilantro, roughly chopped

DIRECTIONS

To make the dosa batter:

1. Put the rice in a bowl, rinse well, and cover with 4 cups of cold water.
2. Put the black gram and fenugreek seeds in a small bowl, rinse well, and add cold water to cover.
3. Leave both to soak for 4-6 hours.
4. Drain the mixtures separately.

5. Put the rice in a food processor or blender. Add 1 cup of cold water and grind to a smooth paste, about 10 minutes. Don't put too much in your food processor or blender. Dividing the mixture into batches will make blending more efficient.

6. Do the same for the dal-fenugreek mixture.

7. In a medium bowl, whisk together the rice and dal-fenugreek pastes. Add water to get a medium-thick consistency.

8. The resulting batter should be about 6 cups in quantity.

9. Place the bowl in a warm place and cover with a kitchen towel. Let it stand for 8 hours to ferment.

10. Stir in the salt. Use the batter immediately, or store it in the refrigerator. It will keep for 1 week.

To make potato filling:

1. Put the ghee or oil in a skillet or karahi over medium heat. Wait for it to shimmer.

2. Add the mustard seeds and cumin seeds. Allow them to crackle and sizzle, about 1 minute.

3. Add the red peppers and onion. Stir-fry until the onions are tender, about 5 minutes.

4. Add the salt, turmeric, asafetida, ginger, curry leaves, garlic and green chilies. Stir and let sizzle for 1 minute.

5. Add potatoes and ½ cup of water.

6. Cook, while stirring, until the liquid is reduced, about 5 minutes.

7. Mash the potatoes coarsely with the back of a ladle.

8. Add the salt and cilantro. Mix well and set aside.

To make the dosas:

1. Set a tawa or griddle over medium heat, and brush it with about 1 teaspoon of vegetable oil.

2. Scoop out ¼ cup of batter and pour it in the center of the tawa.

3. Using the bottom of the ladle, quickly spread the batter outward in a circular motion. The diameter should be about 7 inches.

4. Drizzle ½ teaspoon of oil over the top of the dosa.

5. Let it cook until the outer edges begin to look dry, about 2 minutes. Cook on one side only.

6. With a spatula, carefully loosen the dosa. The bottom should be crisp and beautifully browned. Do not flip it over.

7. Spoon ½ cup of potato filling onto the center of the dosa and flatten the potato mixture slightly.

8. Using the spatula, fold one side of the dosa over the filling like an omelet. You may also fold over both sides to make a cone shape.

9. Serve immediately.

SPICED CAULIFLOWER & POTATOES (ALOO GOBI)

Serves: 8-10 - **Preparation Time:** 10 minutes - **Cooking time:** 15-20 minutes

INGREDIENTS

- 4 cups cauliflower, broken into florets
- 2 teaspoons vegetable oil
- ¼ teaspoon mustard seeds
- ¼ teaspoon cumin seeds
- 5 curry leaves
- 1 green chili, finely chopped
- ½ onion, finely diced
- ½ teaspoon ginger garlic paste
- 1 medium tomato, diced
- 2 medium potatoes, cut into cubes
- 1 celery stalk, diced
- ¼ teaspoon turmeric powder
- ½ teaspoon chili powder
- ¼ teaspoon coriander powder
- ½ teaspoon green mango powder (amchoor)
- 1 teaspoon fenugreek seeds
- ¼ teaspoon garam masala powder
- Salt, to taste
- Cilantro leaves, for garnish

DIRECTIONS

1. Soak the cauliflower florets in hot salted water. Drain, and pat dry with towels.
2. Heat the oil in a nonstick pan. Add mustard seeds, cumin seeds, and curry leaves until they crackle.
3. Add the chopped green chilies, celery, and onion and stir-fry until the onions turn golden brown.
4. Stir in the ginger garlic paste and tomato, and sauté until fragrant.
5. Add potatoes, turmeric, red chili powder, coriander powder, green mango powder, fenugreek seeds, garam masala, and salt. Stir and cover. Simmer over low heat, about 3 minutes.
6. When the potatoes are half cooked, add the cauliflower.
7. Cover and cook for another 3-5 minutes. Sprinkle with water, if needed, to prevent the mixture from drying out.
8. Garnish with cilantro leaves. Serve with rice, poori, or curry.

FRESH WINTER GREENS WITH INDIAN CHEESE (PALAK PANEER)

Serves: 4 - **Preparation Time:** 10 minutes - **Cooking time:** 25 minutes

INGREDIENTS

- 1 bunch spinach (palak)
- 4-5 cloves garlic
- 3 pieces green chili
- 2 medium tomatoes, chopped
- Oil for frying
- 7 ounces Indian cheese (paneer), cut into cubes
- ½ teaspoon cumin seeds
- 1 medium onion, chopped
- 1 tablespoon coriander powder
- ½ teaspoon turmeric powder
- 1 teaspoon garam masala
- 1 tablespoon red chili powder
- Salt, to taste

DIRECTIONS

1. Boil 2 cups of water and add the spinach, garlic, and green chilies, and cook until the spinach has wilted. Remove from the heat immediately and drain well. Set aside some of the boiled liquid for later use.
2. Place the boiled spinach mixture in a blender and add the chopped tomatoes. Blend a little to make a coarse paste. Set aside.
3. Meanwhile, fry the paneer in about 2 tablespoons of oil. Flip it over when one side is browned. Remove the paneer cubes and drain on paper towels.
4. Use the remaining oil in the pan to sauté the cumin seeds and chopped onion. Sauté until onion becomes brown in color.
5. Add the coriander, turmeric masala, and chili powders and stir for 5 minutes.
6. Stir in palak paste and salt. Use drained water to adjust consistency. Mix it well and boil for 2 minutes.
7. Add paneer cubes. Cover and let simmer for 2 minutes.
8. Serve hot with naan or rice.

LEMON RICE

Serves: 4 - **Preparation Time:** 15 minutes   - **Cooking time:** 5-7 minutes

INGREDIENTS

- 2-3 tablespoons vegetable oil or Indian sesame oil (til oil)
- ½ teaspoon mustard seeds (rai/sarson)
- ½ teaspoon black gram or black lentils (urad dal)

- 1 teaspoon split chickpea or Bengal gram (chana dal)
- 5 to 6 curry leaves
- ½ teaspoon grated ginger
- 2 whole dry Kashmiri red chilies, broken into pieces
- ¼ cup peanuts, roasted until golden brown
- ½ teaspoon turmeric powder
- 2 ½ cups cooked rice, cooled down and broken apart to remove lumps
- 1 ½ tablespoons lemon juice
- Salt to taste
- 1 tablespoon cashew nuts, roasted until light golden brown (optional)

DIRECTIONS

1. Heat the oil in a nonstick pan over medium heat and add the mustard seeds. Allow the seeds to crackle.
2. Add the black gram, split chickpea, and curry leaves and sauté for 1 minute.
3. Add the ginger, red chilies, and roasted peanuts. Sauté for 30 seconds.
4. Add the turmeric powder and cooked rice. Cook, stirring constantly, for 2 minutes.
5. Lastly, add lemon juice and salt. Continue cooking while stirring for 2 more minutes.
6. Sprinkle with roasted cashew nuts (optional).
7. Serve hot.

CHICKPEAS IN TOMATO SAUCE (CHANA/CHOLE MASALA)

Serves: 4 - Preparation Time: 20 minutes **- Cooking time:** 20 minutes

INGREDIENTS

- 1 tablespoon coconut oil
- 1 teaspoon cumin seeds
- 1 yellow onion, chopped
- 5 cloves garlic, minced
- 1 tablespoon fresh ginger, peeled and minced
- 1 green Serrano pepper, minced and seeded
- 1 ½ teaspoons garam masala
- 1 ½ teaspoons ground coriander
- ½ teaspoon ground turmeric
- ¾ teaspoon fine-grain sea salt
- ¼ teaspoon cayenne pepper (optional)

- 1 (28-ounce) can whole peeled tomatoes, undrained
- 2 (14-ounce) cans chickpeas, drained and rinsed
- Lemon wedges, for garnish
- Fresh cilantro, chopped, for garnish
- 1 lemon, cut in wedges

DIRECTIONS

1. Heat a large saucepan or dutch oven over medium heat. If a drop of water sizzles when it hits the pan, the temperature is just right.
2. Add the oil, reduce the heat to medium-low, and add the cumin seeds. Oil that is too hot will burn the seeds.
3. Stir the seeds until they turn golden and fragrant, about 1-2 minutes.
4. Adjust the heat to medium.
5. Add the onion, garlic, ginger and serrano pepper. Stir-fry for 5 minutes.
6. Add the garam masala, coriander, turmeric, salt, and cayenne (optional), and cook for 2 more minutes.
7. Add the tomato with its liquid. As you stir, break the tomato into smaller pieces with the spoon.
8. Adjust the heat to medium-high and add the chickpeas.
9. Bring the pot to a simmer and cook for 10 minutes.
10. Adjust the flavor with salt and spices, according to taste.
11. Garnish with cilantro.
12. Serve with steamed rice and lemon wedges.

DEEP FRIED MILK DUMPLINGS IN ROSE SYRUP (GULAB JAMUN)

Serves: 5-7 - **Preparation Time:** 5 minutes plus 2 hours resting time - **Cooking time:** 15 minutes

INGREDIENTS

For dumplings or milk balls:

- 1 cup milk powder
- 3 tablespoons all-purpose flour (maida)
- ⅛ teaspoon baking soda
- Pinch salt
- 1 teaspoon ghee
- 2 tablespoons yogurt or milk
- Oil or ghee, for deep frying

For syrup:

- 1 ½ cups sugar

- 2 cups water

- 1 teaspoon cardamom powder

- 4 drops rose water, or according to taste

- ⅛ teaspoon saffron

DIRECTIONS

1. Sift the milk powder, flour, baking powder, and salt into a bowl.

2. Mix and make a hole in the center.

3. Add the ghee and yogurt, and knead the mixture into a soft, sticky dough. If it's too stiff, gradually add more yogurt.

4. Let it rest.

5. In a saucepan, combine the water and sugar and bring it to a boil.

6. Simmer for 5-8 minutes.

7. Add the cardamom powder, rose essence, and saffron. Mix well.

8. Start making small balls with the dough. The balls or dumplings (jamun) should be about 1 inch in diameter and should not have cracks.

9. Heat the ghee or oil for deep frying over medium heat.

10. Reduce the heat to low and then drop in the jamun.

11. The jamun should sink to the bottom and then slowly rise to the top.

12. Fry until golden brown.

13. Drain well and then immerse into the prepared syrup.

14. Cover and let soak for 2 hours before serving.

CARROT FUDGE (GAJAR KA HALWA)

Serves: 4 - Preparation Time: 5 minutes - **Cooking time:** 1 hour and 20-25 minutes

INGREDIENTS

- 2 tablespoons ghee or neutral cooking oil

- 8 green cardamom pods, seeds only, crushed

- 1 pound carrots, peeled and grated

- 3 cups whole milk

- 1 ¼ cups sugar

- ¼ cup raisins

- Pinch saffron

- ¼ cup unsalted pistachio or roasted cashew nuts, chopped

DIRECTIONS

1. Heat the ghee or oil in a heavy, high-sided skillet or saucepan.

2. Add the crushed cardamom seeds and stir for about 30 seconds, or until fragrant.

3. Add the grated carrots and fry for 3 minutes.

4. Add the milk and bring it to a boil. Boil, stirring constantly, for 5 minutes.

5. Reduce the heat to low and simmer the halwa, uncovered, for about 1 hour.

6. Stir frequently to prevent scorching. The milk should have reduced by over a third by the end of the hour.

7. Stir in the sugar, raisins, and saffron.

8. Turn the heat up to medium and cook, stirring frequently, until the halwa is thick and glossy (15 to 20 minutes)

9. To serve hot, spoon the mixture into bowls and sprinkle with pistachios.

10. To serve cold, press into individual ramekins, muffin tins, or small bowls, and chill. Then, overturn onto serving plates and sprinkle with pistachios or cashews.

TRADITIONAL INDIAN ICE CREAM (KULFI)

Serves: 6 - **Preparation Time:** 5 minutes   - **Cooking time:** 28 minutes

INGREDIENTS

- 2 ½ cups full cream milk
- ½ cup condensed milk
- ¼ cup milk powder
- ½ teaspoon cardamom powder

DIRECTIONS

1. Combine the milk, condensed milk, and milk powder in a deep nonstick pan.

2. Mix well and bring it to a boil. Reduce the heat to medium.

3. Stir in the cardamom powder and simmer for 22 to 25 minutes, scraping the sides down from time to time, stirring occasionally.

4. Remove from the heat and allow it to cool completely.

5. Once it is cooled, pour the mixture into 6 kulfi or ice pop molds and freeze overnight or until firm.

6. Allow them to thaw for a few minutes to make them easy to pull out of molds.

7. Serve immediately.

CREAMY SAFFRON-INFUSED RICE PUDDING (KESARI KHEER)

Serves: 4 - **Preparation Time:** 5 minutes plus 1-2 hours soaking - **Cooking time:** 40 minutes

INGREDIENTS

- ½ cup Bengali sticky rice (Gobindobhog) or jasmine rice
- ⅛ teaspoon saffron (kesar)
- 2 tablespoons milk
- 2 cups milk
- ¼ cup sweetened condensed milk
- ⅓ cup raisins
- ⅓ cup sugar
- 1 tablespoon almonds, slivered
- 2 tablespoons cashew nuts
- 2 tablespoon crushed pistachios, for garnish
- ¼ teaspoon cardamom, crushed

DIRECTIONS

1. Wash and soak the rice for 1-2 hours. Drain.
2. Soak the saffron strands in 2 tablespoons of milk for 1 hour.
3. Pour the milk into a heavy-bottomed pan and bring it to a boil.
4. Add the soaked rice to the boiling milk, stirring constantly.
5. Stir in the saffron-milk mixture.
6. Reduce the heat to medium-low and simmer until the rice is tender but not mushy, about 20-25 minutes. Mix frequently to avoid scorching at the bottom.
7. Add the condensed milk and raisins and continue cooking, stirring often. Add hot water in small amounts, if needed, to prevent the mixture from drying out and scorching.
8. Add sugar, almonds, and cashews, and cook for another 5 minutes.
9. Lastly, add the crushed cardamom. Remove it from the heat and let it cool.
10. Serve lukewarm or chilled (the flavor is enhanced when chilled) and garnished with crushed pistachio nuts.

BUTTERY FUDGE SQUARES (BURFI/BARFI)

Serves: 9 - **Preparation Time:** 5 minutes - **Cooking time:** 15 to 20 minutes

INGREDIENTS

- ¼ cup ghee or butter, plus more for greasing
- ¾ cup all-purpose flour (maida)
- 1 cup sugar
- ⅓ cup water

- A few drops or a pinch yellow food coloring

DIRECTIONS

1. Prepare a tray, about 1 ½-inch to 2 inches deep. Grease with ghee or butter. Set aside.
2. Melt the ghee in a nonstick pan over medium low heat.
3. Add flour and stir until fragrant, then transfer to a bowl.
4. Using the same pan over medium heat, mix the sugar, water and food coloring together.
5. Cook until 1-string consistency is attained. To test: dip a wooden spoon into the syrup and let cool for a few seconds (hot syrup can scald). When cooled to a safe temperature, place between thumb and forefinger. Gently separate fingers. If a string of syrup is formed that does not break, your syrup is ready.
6. Turn off the heat immediately and add the flour mixture, stirring continuously.
7. Keep mixing for 3 to 5 minutes, until the mixture thickens.
8. Pour into the greased tray and smooth the top with a spatula.
9. Let set for 15 to 30 minutes.
10. Cut it into squares and serve.

METHI MALAI PANEER (CREAMY FENUGREEK AND SPINACH WITH CHEESE)

Servings: 8

INGREDIENTS

- 4 tbsp. canola oil
- 1/2 cup cashews
- 1/4 cup garlic, minced
- 1 small red onion, minced
- 1 teaspoon cumin seeds
- 1 pound baby spinach
- 2/3 pound fenugreek, trimmed and roughly chopped, or 4 cups frozen chopped fenugreek, defrosted
- 1/2 pound paneer, coarsely grated
- 1 cup frozen peas
- 1/2 cup heavy cream
- 4 tbsp. unsalted butter
- 1 teaspoon red chile powder, such as cayenne
- 1 teaspoon garam masala

- 1 teaspoon ground coriander
- 1 teaspoon ground cumin
- 1 teaspoon ground turmeric
- 6 canned whole, peeled tomatoes, drained and crushed by hand
- kosher salt, to taste
- naan, for serving (optional)

DIRECTIONS

1. Warmth oil in a 12" skillet over medium-high. Make cashews and cumin seeds until fragrant and seeds start to pop, 1-2 moments. Add garlic and onion; cook until golden, 3-4 moments. Add spinach and fenugreek; cook until wilted, 2-3 moments. Add paneer, peas, cream, butter, cayenne, garam masala, coriander, cumin, turmeric, tomatoes, salt, and 1/4 cup drinking water; boil. Reduce warmth to medium; make, covered, and stirring sometimes, until mixture is somewhat thickened about 25 moments. Serve with naan, if you want.

DAIKON CURRY

Servings: 8

INGREDIENTS

- 4 tbsp. canola oil
- 1 teaspoon ajwain (carom) seeds
- 1/4 cup garlic, minced
- 2 pounds . daikon with greens, peeled and cut into 1/2" pieces, greens trimmed and roughly chopped
- 1 teaspoon ground coriander
- 1 medium yellow onion, roughly chopped
- 1 teaspoon ground cumin
- 1 teaspoon ground turmeric
- 1/2 teaspoon red chile powder, such as cayenne
- 2 teaspoons amchur (green mango) powder
- kosher salt, to taste
- chapatis, for serving (optional)

DIRECTIONS

1. Warmth oil in a 12" skillet over medium-high high temperature. Make carom seeds until they pop, 1-2 a few minutes. Add garlic and onion; cook until golden, 5-7 minutes. Mix in daikon and its own leaves, the coriander, cumin, turmeric, and chile powder. Reduce high temperature to medium-low; make, covered, and stirring sometimes, until daikon is certainly tender about 20 minutes. Mix in amchur and salt; serve with chapatis, if you want.

RAJASTHANI WHITE CHICKEN CURRY

Servings: 8

INGREDIENTS

- 1/2 cup desiccated coconut
- 2 tbsp. white poppy seeds
- 50 whole white peppercorns
- 40 cashews
- 1 1/2 tablespoons pumpkins seeds
- 20 green cardamom pods
- 1 cup ghee
- 2 teaspoons kala jeera (black cumin)
- 12 whole cloves
- 8 black cardamom pods, cracked
- 4 indian or regular bay leaves
- 1 cup cinnamon
- 8 small green thai chiles or 2 serranos, halved
- 6 tablespoons garlic, minced
- 2 medium yellow onions, minced
- 2 pieces 1 (2") ginger, peeled and minced
- 2 (2 1/2–3-lb.) chicken, cut into 8 pieces, skin removed
- 1 1/2 cups plain, full-fat yogurt
- 1 1/2 whole milk
- 1 teaspoon ground mace
- kosher salt, to taste
- 4 tbsp. roughly chopped cilantro, for garnish

DIRECTIONS

1. Grind coconut, poppy seeds, pumpkin seeds, 15 white peppercorns, 10 cashews, and the green cardamom in a spice grinder right into a powder; set aside.

2. Melt ghee in a 6-qt. saucepan over medium-high heat. Make staying peppercorns, the Kala jeera, cloves, dark cardamom, bay leaves, and cinnamon until fragrant and seeds start to pop, 1-2 mins. Add chiles, garlic, onion, and ginger; prepare until golden, 8-10 mins. Add chicken, yogurt, milk, mace, and salt; boil. Reduce heat to moderate and mix in reserved spice powder; make, covered somewhat, and stirring sometimes, until chicken is prepared through, 20-22 mins. Using tongs, transfer chicken to a serving platter. Mix staying cashews into sauce; simmer until somewhat thickened, 4-6 a few minutes; spoon over chicken and garnish with cilantro.

CREAMY CASHEW INDIAN BUTTER PANEER...WITH FRIED PANEER!

Servings: 12

INGREDIENTS

- 1/4 cup coconut oil or ghee or butter
- 2 (14-ounce) cans coconut milk lite or regular
- 1 1/2 cups roasted cashews
- 1 pound paneer cheese cubed
- 2 (6 ounce) tomato paste can
- 1/2 cup greek yogurt or 1/4 cup more coconut milk for vegans
- 1 a small sweet onion diced
- 1/4 cup garlic minced or grated
- 2 tablespoons fresh ginger grated
- 1 1/2 tablespoons spicy curry powder
- 2 teaspoons 1-2 thai red curry paste i used 2
- 2 tablespoons 1-2 garam masala i used 1
- 1 teaspoon turmeric
- 2 teaspoons cayenne pepper or to taste
- 1/2 teaspoon salt
- 2 teaspoons saffron optional
- 2 cups 1-2 broccoli florets
- chopped cilantro for topping
- steamed rice for serving
- fresh naan for serving

DIRECTIONS

1. Heat a huge skillet over medium temperature and add 1 tablespoon coconut essential oil (or ghee). Once popular, add the cubed paneer in batches and make about 2 minutes per part or until sharp. Remove from heat and drain in writing towels. Do it again with any staying paneer. Reserve the skillet and arrange the paneer apart.*

2. To a food processor chip or high powered blender, add the cashews and coconut milk. Mix on high until totally smooth and silky, about 3-4 mins. Add the tomato paste, yogurt, and 1/2 cup water. Mix until smooth. Reserve.

3. To the same skillet, you fried the paneer, add the rest of the tablespoon of oil. Once popular, add the onion, garlic, and ginger, cook about 5-8 mins or before the onion is smooth and gently caramelized.

Add the curry powder, thai reddish colored curry paste, garam masala, turmeric, cayenne, and salt. Cook about a minute and then mix in the cashew/coconut blend. Bring the sauce to a mild boil and if it appears too solid for your liking, mix in drinking water or coconut milk to slim. Once the sauce reaches your desired consistency, mix in the crispy paneer and saffron if using. Add the broccoli and make until warmed through and the sauce thickened somewhat about five minutes. Remove from heat and serve over a bed of warm rice sprinkled with cut cilantro. Also, keep in mind the naan for dipping!

PORK VINDALOO

Servings: 12

INGREDIENTS

- 1 1/2 cups 12-14 garlic
- 2 tbsp. hot paprika
- 2 tbsp. sugar
- 2 tbsp. sweet paprika
- 2 teaspoons brown mustard seeds
- 1 1/2 tablespoons kosher salt
- 4 tbsp. tomato paste
- 1 cup distilled white vinegar
- 1/2 cup canola oil
- 2 medium red onions, chopped (1 1/2 cups)
- 1 teaspoon crushed red chile flakes
- 4 pounds . pork shoulder, cut into 1/2-inch pieces (5 cups)

DIRECTIONS

1. Make the sauce: In a meals processor chip or blender, combine the garlic, both paprikas, mustard seeds, sugars, salt, tomato paste, vinegar, and 1/4 glass water; purée until soft.
2. In a sizable cast-iron skillet, heat the oil over medium-high. Add the onion and chile flakes, and make, stirring, before the onion is golden dark brown, about 5-6 mins. Add the pork and the puréed sauce. Stir well to layer the pork, cover, decrease temperature to low, and make before pork is falling aside and the sauce is usually solid and lush about 45 minutes.

REBECCA COLLERTON

Servings: 10

INGREDIENTS

- olive oil

- 12 scallions, cut into 1-inch pieces
- 4 jalapeños, seeds removed if desired
- 2 1-inch piece ginger, peeled, chopped
- 2 tablespoons fresh lemon juice
- 12 garlic cloves
- 2 tablespoons garam masala
- 2 teaspoons ground coriander
- 1 teaspoon ground cumin
- 1 teaspoon cayenne pepper
- 4 pounds ground beef (20% fat)
- 2 large eggs, beaten to blend
- 6 tablespoons plain yogurt
- 1 1/2 tablespoons kosher salt
- 1/2 cup olive oil
- 8 medium onions, chopped
- 20 garlic cloves, crushed
- 2 1/2-inch piece ginger, peeled, chopped
- 6 dried chiles de árbol
- 2 1/2 tablespoons curry powder
- 2 1/2 tablespoons ground cumin
- 2 1/2 tablespoons ground turmeric
- 6 tablespoons ground coriander
- 2 teaspoons black peppercorns
- 2 ounces 14.5- can crushed tomatoes
- 2 bay leaves
- 2 tablespoons kosher salt, plus more
- 2 tablespoons fresh lemon juice
- 1 teaspoon cayenne pepper
- leaf cilantro with tender stems (for serving)

DIRECTIONS

1. Preheat oven to 400°. Gently brush a rimmed baking sheet with essential oil. Purée scallions, jalapeños, garlic, ginger, lemon juice, garam masala, coriander, cumin, and cayenne in a blender until clean. Transfer blend to a huge bowl and put beef, egg, yogurt, and salt. Mix together with your hands until the blend is homogenous and begins to become extremely sticky like sausage meats, about 1 minute. Utilizing a 2-oz. ice cream scoop to part if you want, roll beef blend into golfing ball-size portions and put on a baking sheet, spacing 1" apart (you ought to have about 24). Drizzle meatballs with an increase

of essential oil and bake until browned at the top and cooked through, 20-25 minutes.

2. Meanwhile, heat essential oil in a huge Dutch oven or additional heavy pot over moderate. Add onions, garlic, and ginger and prepare, stirring frequently, until onions are translucent and beginning to brown, 8-10 minutes. Mix in chiles, curry powder, cumin, turmeric, coriander, and peppercorns. Cook, stirring frequently until mixture is quite fragrant and spices start to adhere to the pot, about 2 mins. Add tomatoes, stirring and scraping bottom level of the pot, and provide to a boil. Add bay leaf, 1 Tbsp. salt, and 2 cups water; go back to a boil. Reduce temperature and simmer until tastes have melded, 25-30 minutes.

3. Let curry sauce awesome slightly, after transfer to a blender; blend until very clean. Get rid of any bits staying in the pot and transfer curry sauce back again to the pot. Mix in lemon juice and cayenne; flavor sauce and time of year with an increase of salt if needed.

4. Lightly nestle cooked meatballs into sauce, bring to a simmer, and cook until meatballs are heated completely, 10-15 minutes. Serve topped with cilantro.

5. Do Forward: Meatballs and sauce could be made one day ahead. Let great; transfer to an airtight container and chill. Carefully reheat meatballs in sauce, covered, thinning with drinking water if the sauce is normally too thick.

SAAG PANEER

Servings: 8

INGREDIENTS

- 16 cups milk
- 12 tbsp. ghee or canola oil
- 1/2 cup garlic, chopped
- 1/2 cup fresh lemon juice
- one 1-inch piece ginger, peeled and chopped
- 2 serrano chile, stemmed and chopped
- 12 cups finely chopped spinach
- kosher salt
- 12 tbsp. heavy cream
- 1 teaspoon garam masala
- 1/2 teaspoon cayenne
- indian flatbread or rice, for serving

DIRECTIONS

1. Make the cheese: Range a colander with 8 layers of cheesecloth, draping it over the sides, and occur a sink. In a big, nonstick pot over medium-high warmth, provide the milk to a complete boil, stirring

frequently with a wooden spoon to avoid it from scorching underneath. Mix in the lemon juice, then lower heat to medium-low and prepare without stirring simply until large curds form about 30 secs. Remove from heat and reserve, without disturbing for 2 minutes, after that pour the milk mix into the colander. Collect the corners of cheesecloth jointly and carefully squeeze out a few of the surplus liquid. Tie the contrary corners of the cheesecloth jointly to produce a sack, and hang it from a sizable kitchen spoon suspended over a deep bowl. Reserve at room temperature before the excess liquid has completely drained from the cheese, about 1 1/2 hours. Transfer the sack to a plate, untie the cheesecloth, and loosely drape the corners over the cheese. Place a sizable heavy pot along with the cheese, then reserve at room temperatures to compress for thirty minutes more. Take away the pot and unwrap the cheese. Cut into 1/2-inch-by-1-inch parts.

2. In a 12-inch nonstick skillet, heat the ghee over medium. Employed in batches, add the cheese and fry until golden dark brown, about 6 minutes. Utilizing a slotted spoon, transfer the cheese to a plate and reserve; reserve the skillet with ghee.

3. Make the spinach: In a blender, combine the garlic, ginger, chile, and 1/4 cup drinking water; purée into a simple paste. Come back the skillet with ghee to the stove, and warmth over medium-high. Add the ginger-garlic paste and make, stirring, until fragrant, about 30 mere seconds. Add the spinach, salt to flavor, and cook, stirring frequently, before spinach wilts, about 1 minute. Decrease the warmth to medium-low, cover, and cook, stirring often, before spinach is quite soft, about quarter-hour. Mix in the cream, garam masala, and cayenne. Add the cheese to the skillet, cover, and continue cooking food before liquid thickens and spinach is definitely soft, about a quarter-hour even more. Serve with flatbread or rice.

RICK MARTINEZ

Servings: 10
INGREDIENTS

- cup yogurt ½ whole-milk Greek yogurt
- 1/2 cup garlic grated
- 2 tablespoons ginger finely grated ginger
- 1 1/2 tablespoons salt kosher salt
- 2 tablespoons fenugreek leaves (optional)
- 4 pounds chicken thighs boneless skinless chicken thighs
- cup butter ½ (1 stick) cultured or unsalted butter divided
- 1 cup cinnamon 3-inch cinnamon
- 10 cardamom green cardamom pods
- 2 whole clove

- 1 1/2 tablespoons fenugreek seeds (optional)
- 4 onions medium onions sliced
- 4 serrano chiles split lengthwise
- salt Kosher salt
- 1/2 cup garlic grated
- 2 tablespoons ginger finely grated ginger
- 2 tablespoons fenugreek leaves (optional)
- 2 tablespoons garam masala
- 2 teaspoons paprika
- teaspoon turmeric ½ ground turmeric
- 4 cans tomatoes 28-ounce whole peeled tomatoes
- cup heavy cream ½ heavy cream
- cilantro Chopped cilantro steamed basmati rice and naan (for serving)

DIRECTIONS

1. Whisk yogurt, garlic, fenugreek leaves, if using, ginger, and salt in a moderate bowl. Add poultry and toss to layer. Cover and chill for at least one hour or more to 3.

2. Melt 4 Tbsp. butter in a sizable wide pot over moderate heat. Make cinnamon, cardamom pods, clove, and fenugreek seeds, if using, stirring, until somewhat darker and fragrant, 1-2 mins. Add onion and chiles, period with salt, and make, stirring sometimes, until onion can be golden and starting to caramelize, 8-10 mins. Add garlic and ginger and prepare, stirring, until extremely fragrant and ginger begins to carefully turn golden and sticks to bottom level of the pot, 2-3 mins. Add fenugreek leaves, if using, garam masala, paprika, and turmeric and prepare, stirring, until extremely fragrant, about 1 minute. Add tomatoes, splitting up into parts with a spoon, and prepare until brick reddish colored and the majority of the liquid can be evaporated for about 1 minute. Utilizing a potato masher or large spoon, smash tomatoes and continue steadily to simmer, uncovered, until sauce may be the consistency of a heavy ragù, 40-50 mins. Discard cinnamon stay (leave other entire spices).

3. Transfer blend to a blender and purée until even. Cut staying 4 Tbsp. butter into parts. Add butter and cream to blender and purée until creamy; period with salt. Come back sauce to the pot and provide to a simmer.

4. Meanwhile, preheat the broiler. Arrange chicken within a layer on a cable rack set in the foil-lined rimmed baking sheet. Broil until chicken begins to brown in areas (you won't be cooked through), 7-8 minutes per aspect. When cool more than enough to take care of, cut into ¾" parts. Add poultry to simmering sauce, cover, and cook until poultry is cooked through, 8-10 minutes.

5. Best chicken and sauce with cilantro. Serve with rice and naan alongside.

6. Do Ahead: Butter poultry can be produced 3 days forward. Let great; cover and chill.

ROASTED EGGPLANT AND CRISPY KALE WITH YOGURT

Servings: 10

INGREDIENTS

- 4 medium italian eggplants (about 1 1/2 pounds total), quartered lengthwise, cut crosswise into 1-inch pieces
- 1/2 cup vegetable oil
- kosher salt
- 1 teaspoon ground cumin
- 12 tuscan kale leaves, ribs and stems removed, leaves coarsely torn
- 2 teaspoons dried mangos powder (amchoor; optional)
- 2 medium persian cucumbers
- 2 cups plain whole-milk greek yogurt
- 2 teaspoons fresh lemon juice
- 2 garlic cloves, finely grated
- 4 cups cherry tomatoes, halved
- olive oil (for drizzling)

DIRECTIONS

1. Preheat oven to 450°. Toss eggplants with veggie essential oil on a rimmed baking sheet; time of year with salt. Roast, tossing halfway through, until eggplants are charred in places and tender, 20-25 moments. Remove from oven, sprinkle with mango powder (if using) and cumin, and toss to coat.
2. Meanwhile, heat a dry out a large skillet, ideally cast iron, over medium-large. Add kale, arranging to squeeze in an individual even layer (function in batches if required), and cook, turning sometimes until charred in places and crisp, about 4 minutes.
3. Grate cucumber about the moderate holes of a box grater; squeeze out extra liquid together with your hands and transfer to a moderate bowl. Blend in yogurt, lemon juice, and garlic; time of year with salt.
4. Toss tomatoes with an excellent pinch of salt and a drizzle of essential olive oil in a moderate bowl. Spoon yogurt combination onto a platter and coating eggplants, kale, and tomatoes at the top. Drizzle with even more olive oil.

ROTI (INDIAN WHOLE WHEAT FLATBREAD)

Servings: 11

INGREDIENTS

- 2 cups atta (chapati) flour, plus more for rolling
- 1/2 teaspoon kosher salt
- 3/4 teaspoon . corn oils or canola oil, plus more for shaping
- melted ghee, for brushing

DIRECTIONS

1. In a moderate bowl, use the hands to mix the flour, oil, and salt. Add 1 glass water and combine, pinching and kneading the dough as you function. Add yet another 1/4 cup of drinking water and continue steadily to knead and convert the dough in the bowl, scraping up the loose flour from the sides and bottom level. Continue before dough is smooth no much longer sticky. (If the dough appears dry, soon add up to 1/4 cup more drinking water, 1 tablespoon at the same time, blending well between each addition.)

2. Divide the dough into 4 equal parts. Rub a little of essential oil on your own hands, and roll each piece right into a log, about 2 inches heavy. Pinch off golf ball-sized pieces, about 1 1/4 ounce each, and roll each right into a ball. Cover the balls with a dish towel and reserve.

3. Fill a little bowl with atta flour, then lightly dirt a chakra or countertop with more flour. Dealing with one ball of dough at the same time, flatten the ball right into a thick disk. Dredge the disk of dough in the plate of flour, then make use of a belan or rolling pin to roll the ball right into a disc about 6-6 1/2 inches in diameter.

4. Meanwhile, at high temperature, a Tava or a moderate nonstick or cast iron dry out skillet over moderate to medium-high high temperature. When the pan is quite scorching, place one roti in the skillet. When you find small white spots type on the top of the dough, about 45 seconds, make use of tongs or your fingertips to flip, then make on the remaining aspect until it bubbles just a little and light brown areas form, 20-30 secs more.

5. Take away the roti from the pan and stick it directly over the gas flame; let make until it puffs and swells, after that, using tongs, quickly flip it backward and forwards for some seconds to keep puffing and getting brownish spots all over.

6. Transfer the roti to a serving dish and instantly brush 1 or both sides with ghee. Cover with a clean kitchen towel when you continue rolling and cooking food all of that other roti this way. Serve warm.

SAMBAR (SOUTH INDIAN VEGETABLE STEW)

Servings: 12

INGREDIENTS

- 1 cup toor dal (yellow pigeon peas), rinsed, soaked 30 minutes, and drained

- 1 cup coconut or canola oil
- 2 small red onions, cut into 1" pieces
- 2 pieces 1 (2") ginger, peeled and mashed into a paste
- 1 cup garlic, mashed into a paste
- 8 small green thai chiles or 2 serranos, chopped
- 4 drumsticks, trimmed and cut into 2" pieces
- 4 medium carrots, quartered lengthwise and cut into 2" pieces
- 4 medium yukon gold potatoes, peeled and cut into 1" pieces
- 4 plum tomatoes, chopped
- 1 cup sambar masala
- 6 tbsp. fresh or frozen grated coconut
- 6 tbsp. tamarind paste
- 2 tbsp. ground cumin
- 2 teaspoons ground turmeric
- 20 small okra, trimmed and halved crosswise
- kosher salt, to taste
- 1 1/2 tablespoons black mustard seeds
- 20 fresh or frozen curry leaves
- 10 chiles de árbol
- 1/2 cup cilantro leaves
- cooked white rice, for serving (optional)

DIRECTIONS

1. Bring 1/3 glass toor dal and 4 cups drinking water to a boil in a 6-qt. saucepan. Reduce heat to moderate and make until dal is quite tender about one hour. Transfer to a bowl; reserve.

2. Wipe pan clean; temperature half the essential oil over medium-high. Make garlic, onion, and ginger until slightly caramelized, 8-10 mins. Add green chiles, drumsticks, carrots, potatoes, tomatoes, and 3 1/2 cups water; boil. Reduce temperature to moderate; simmer until vegetables are tender, 15-20 mins. Mix in reserved toor dal, the sambar masala, coconut, tamarind paste, cumin, turmeric, okra, and salt; simmer until okra is definitely tender, 10-15 minutes.

3. Heat remaining oil within an 8" skillet over medium-high; prepare mustard seeds, curry leaves, and chiles de árbol until seeds pop, 1-2 mins; pour over the sambar and garnish with cilantro. Serve with rice privately if you like.

TANDOORI CHICKEN DRUMSTICKS WITH CILANTRO-SHALLOT RELISH

Servings: 10

INGREDIENTS

- 2 tablespoons sweet paprika
- 2 tablespoons garam masala
- 2 tablespoons ground cumin
- 1 teaspoon ground turmeric
- 2 tablespoons finely grated peeled fresh ginger
- 2 tablespoons ground coriander
- 1/2 cup garlic
- 1/2 cup fat-free greek-style yogurt
- 2 tablespoons lemon juice
- 1 cup canola oil
- kosher salt
- freshly ground pepper
- 24 chicken drumsticks
- 1 1/2 cups coarsely chopped cilantro
- 2 small shallots
- 6 tablespoons distilled white vinegar

DIRECTIONS

1. Preheat the oven to 450 degrees F. Established a rack on each of 2 large baking sheets. In a little skillet, toast the paprika, garam masala, cumin, coriander, and turmeric over moderately low high temperature, stirring, until fragrant, about 2 a few minutes. Transfer the spices to a moderate bowl and cool somewhat. Mix in the ginger, garlic, yogurt, lemon juice, and 2 tablespoons of the essential oil and period with salt and pepper. Make two or three 3 slashes in each drumstick. In a sizable bowl, toss the poultry with 2 tablespoons of the canola essential oil and period with salt and pepper. Add the spiced yogurt and rub it onto the poultry. Arrange the poultry on the racks, departing 2 inches between your pieces. Roast for 45 minutes, turning occasionally before the chicken is golden dark brown, and prepared through. Light the broiler and broil the poultry 6 inches from heat for about five minutes, until gently charred and sharp. In a little bowl, mix the cilantro, shallot, vinegar, and the rest of the 1/4 glass of oil; time of year with salt. Serve with the poultry. Looking for more poultry recipes? Try our selections of chicken white meat recipes, chicken casserole quality recipes, and quality recipes for leftover chicken.

VEGGIE AND RICOTTA MUFFINS

Cooking time: 30minutes - **Servings:** 2

INGREDIENTS:

- 4 eggs
- 4 slices bacon, cooked and crumbled
- 1 tablespoon sundried tomato in olive oil, chopped
- 4 medium mushrooms, chopped
- 1 tablespoon fresh basil, chopped
- ¼ teaspoon onion salt
- ¼ teaspoon garlic opt, chopped
- ¼ cup parmesan, shredded
- ½ teaspoon Italian seasoning

DIRECTIONS

1. Preheat the oven to 400 F.
2. Spray muffin pan with cooking spray.
3. Mix all the ingredients in a bowl until well combined. Divide the batter among cups and bake for 25-30 minutes.
4. Let rest for couple of minutes before serving.

SPICY BACON AND EGG CUPS KETO

Cooking time: 30 minutes - **Servings:** 2

INGREDIENTS:

- 4 oz cheddar cheese, shredded
- 3 oz cream cheese
- 4 chili peppers, de-seeded and sliced
- 12 strips bacon
- 8 eggs, beaten
- ½ teaspoon garlic powder
- ½ teaspoon onion powder
- Salt and pepper, to taste

DIRECTIONS

1. Preheat the oven to 375F. Preheat a non stick skillet over medium heat. Add bacon and cook until slightly browned. Transfer to a plate.
2. Mix cream cheese, eggs, garlic powder, onion powder, salt and pepper in a bowl.
3. Prepare muffin tins and grease with cooking spray.
4. Par-cook bacon so it's semi crisp but still pliable. Save bacon grease to add to mixture.
5. Use a hand mixer, to mix all the other ingredients (except cheddar and 1 jalapeno) together.

6. Grease wells of muffin tin, then place cooked bacon around the edges. Pour the egg mixture into the muffin cups.

7. Top with cheddar cheese and chili pepper ring. Cook for 20-25 minutes. Let cool before serving.

BREAKFAST BOWL UPMA

Cooking time: 15 minutes - **Servings:** 2

INGREDIENTS:

- 7 oz cauliflower
- 2 tablespoons ghee
- 1 teaspoon ginger
- ½ onion
- 4 curry leaves
- 1 tablespoon cumin seeds
- 1 tablespoon mustard seeds
- 1 green chilly, chopped
- Chopped coriander, for serving
- Salt, to taste

DIRECTIONS

1. Add cauliflower florets to a food processor and blend to get rice consistency.

2. Preheat ghee in a deep skillet over medium heat. Add cumin and mustard seeds. Add onion, curry leaves, ginger and chilli, season with salt. Cook for about 3-4 minutes.

3. Add cauliflower rice and cook for 2 minutes. Add 1 cup water and cover the skillet, cook for 10 minutes, stirring from time to time.

4. Serve topped with coriander.

MEAT AND VEGGIE STUFFED OMELET

Cooking time: 5 minutes - **Servings:** 2

INGREDIENTS:

- 4 eggs
- 1 cup cooked chicken meat
- 1 cup frozen vegetables mix
- ¼ teaspoon salt
- ¼ teaspoon red chili powder
- 1 green chili, chopped

- ½ onion, chopped
- 1 teaspoon coriander
- 1 tablespoon butter
- A pinch of turmeric

DIRECTIONS

1. Beat eggs, salt, chilli powder, turmeric, coriander, onion and green chilli in a bowl.
2. Preheat butter in a skillet over medium heat. Add chicken and frozen vegetables, cook for about 3-4 minutes.
3. Add the beaten egg mixture, fry the eggs until set on one side. Fold the eggs and cook for about 2-3 minutes more. Enjoy!

BACON BRUSSELS SPROUTS

Cooking time: 15 minutes - **Servings:** 4

INGREDIENTS:

- 12 oz Brussels sprouts
- 4 slices bacon, chopped
- 2 garlic cloves
- 1 teaspoon paprika
- 1 tablespoon olive oil
- 1 teaspoon salt
- 1/2 teaspoon pepper

DIRECTIONS

1. Preheat a non stick skillet over medium heat. Add bacon and cook until slightly browned. Transfer to a plate.
2. Add olive oil to the skillet, add sprouts, salt, pepper and paprika. Cook for about 5 minutes. Add garlic and cook for 5 minutes more.
3. Add bacon to the skillet and cook for 1 minute. Serve.

CAULIFLOWER TIKKIS

Cooking time: 15 minutes - **Servings:** 4

INGREDIENTS:

- 8 cauliflower florets
- 1 onion, chopped
- 1/4 cup coriander leaves, chopped

- 2 green chilies, chopped
- 3 tablespoons gram flour
- 1 tablespoons coriander powder
- 1 teaspoon cumin powder
- 1/2 teaspoon black pepper
- 1/2 teaspoon turmeric powder
- 1 teaspoon red chili powder
- 4 tablespoons mustard oil
- Salt, to taste

DIRECTIONS

1. Bring a pan of water to a boil and add salt. Add cauliflower and simmer for 5-6 minutes. Drain and grate the florets to flour texture.
2. Add cauliflower, onion, coriander, green chilies, flour, coriander, cumin, turmeric, chili powder, salt and pepper to a bowl and mix well to combine.
3. Preheat oil in a skillet over medium heat. Shape the mixture into patties and fry in the skillet and fry until browned on both sides.

MULTI FILLINGS EGG MUFFINS

Cooking time: 25 minutes - **Servings:** 6

INGREDIENTS:

- 12 eggs
- 2 scallions, chopped
- 5 oz chorizo, cooked
- 6 oz cheese, shredded
- 2 tablespoons red pesto
- Salt and pepper, to taste

DIRECTIONS

1. Preheat the oven to 350°F. Prepare muffin tin and grease with cooking spray.
2. Mix all the batter ingredients in a bowl and divide among muffin cups.
3. Bake for 15-20 minutes.

CHEESE AND MEAT CHIPS

Cooking time: 10 minutes - **Servings:** 4

INGREDIENTS:

- 3 oz salami, 20 slices
- 4 oz parmesan cheese, grated
- 1 teaspoon paprika powder

DIRECTIONS

1. Preheat the oven to 450°F. Prepare a baking sheet and line it with parchment paper.
2. Place the salami slices on the baking sheet. Add the shredded cheese on top of each slice, sprinkle with paprika powder.
3. Bake until the cheese turns golden brown. Serve.

ROASTED MIXED NUTS

Cooking time: 5 minutes - **Servings:** 16

INGREDIENTS:

- 3 cups raw nuts (cashews, almonds and Brazil nuts)
- 1 teaspoon sea salt
- 1 tablespoon cinnamon
- 1 teaspoon vanilla essence
- 1 cup granulated Erythritol
- 1/4 cup water

DIRECTIONS

1. Preheat a deep pot over medium heat. Add Erythritol, sea salt, cinnamon and water and mix to combine. Heat up, stirring occasionally.
2. Add the nuts and mix to combine. Cook for about 2-3 minutes, stirring often.
3. Let rest for 1-2 minutes before serving.

KURKURE PANEER SLICES

Cooking time: 5 minutes - **Servings:** 8

INGREDIENTS:

- 3 ½ oz paneer, sliced
- 3 tablespoons breadcrumbs
- 2 tablespoons ground flaxseeds
- 1 teaspoon turmeric powder
- 2 teaspoons red chili powder
- 1 teaspoon cumin powder
- 1 teaspoon garam masala

- 1 teaspoon chat masala
- Salt, to taste
- Oil, for frying

DIRECTIONS

1. Toss paneer in 2 teaspoons corn flour and salt.
2. Mix flaxseeds, turmeric powder, red chilli powder, cumin powder, garam masala and salt in a bowl.
3. Add water and mix well until lump free batter is formed.
4. Preheat oil in a pan, dip each paneer slice into batter and then dip into breadcrumbs. Fry until brown on all sides.

CHEESY TAMATAR SALAD

Cooking time: 5 minutes - **Servings:** 2

INGREDIENTS:

- 1 cucumber, chopped
- 1 plum tomato, chopped
- 1 red onion, sliced
- 1 lime, juiced
- 3 oz paneer, cubed
- 2 green chillies
- 1 teaspoon chat masala
- Fresh chopped coriander

DIRECTIONS

1. Mix cucumber, tomato, onion and paneer in a bowl.
2. Add coriander and sprinkle with lime juice, toss to coat.
3. Add chat masala and stir to combine. Serve.

CRUNCHY BROCCOLI TOFU SALAD

Cooking time: 15 minutes - **Servings:** 4

INGREDIENTS:

- 1 (14 oz) package extra-firm tofu
- 1 head of broccoli, florets chopped
- 2 tablespoons vegetable oil
- 2 scallions, sliced
- 1 hot chili, sliced

- Salt and pepper, to taste

For the Dressing:

- 1 tablespoon rice vinegar
- ½ teaspoon soy sauce
- ¼ teaspoon sugar
- 2 tablespoons sesame oil
- 2 teaspoons sesame seeds, toasted

DIRECTIONS

1. Preheat the oven to 400 F. Toss broccoli florets with 1 tablespoon vegetable oil, salt and pepper. Place on a baking sheet and bake for about 5 minutes, remove from the oven. Reduce oven heat to 350 F.
2. Preheat the remaining oil in a pan. Add tofu and sprinkle with salt and pepper. Add to the pan and cook for about 1-2 minutes per all sides.
3. Transfer to the baking sheet and cook for 8-10 minutes.
4. Mix all dressing ingredients in a bowl. Mix broccoli, tofu, scallions and chili, top with dressing, toss to coat. Serve.

SAUSAGE STIR FRY

Cooking time: 25 minutes - **Servings:** 4

INGREDIENTS:

- 10 chicken sausages, sliced
- 2 tablespoons oil
- 1 tablespoon butter
- 10 garlic cloves, crushed
- 2 onions, sliced
- 1 bell pepper, sliced
- 2 teaspoons red chili pepper
- 1 teaspoon garam masala
- 1 teaspoon pepper powder
- 1 teaspoon vinegar
- ½ cup tomato ketchup
- Salt, to taste

DIRECTIONS

1. Preheat oil and butter in a pan. Add crushed garlic and cook for about 1 minute.
2. Add onions and salt. Cook until browned. Add sausage and cook for 8-10 minutes.
3. Add peppers and sauté for 2-3 minutes. Add chili powder and stir well.

4. Add ketchup and toss to coat. Add vinegar, garam masala powder and pepper powder, mix well to combine. Serve.

ZUCCHINI CHEESE AND GARLIC BREADSTICKS

Cooking time: 40 minutes - **Servings:** 2

INGREDIENTS:

- 4 zucchinis, grated
- ⅓ cup parmesan cheese, grated
- ⅓ cup cheddar cheese, grated
- ½ cup mozzarella cheese, grated
- 1 egg
- 1 tablespoon garlic powder
- 1 teaspoon pepper
- ½ teaspoon red pepper flakes
- ½ teaspoon salt

DIRECTIONS

1. Preheat the oven to 400°F.
2. Mix grated zucchini, parmesan cheese, garlic powder, pepper, red pepper flakes, salt, and egg in a bowl. Mix well to combine.
3. Line the baking sheet with parchment paper. Spread the mixture evenly on the baking sheet, about ½ inch thick.
4. Bake for 35-40 minutes. Top with cheddar and mozzarella cheese. Bake for 10 minutes more.
5. Let cool and slice into sticks. Serve.

SPINACH YOGURT CHEESE DIP WITH VEGGIES

Cooking time: 2 minutes - **Servings:** 8

INGREDIENTS:

- 2 cups fresh spinach
- 2 tablespoons Greek yogurt
- 3/4 cup cheddar cheese, shredded
- 1/4 cup parmesan cheese, shredded

- 1/4 teaspoon garlic powder
- 1/2 teaspoon salt

DIRECTIONS

1. Add spinach to a skillet and cook over medium heat for 2-3 minutes, stirring frequently.
2. Transfer to a plate and let cool slightly. Chop the spinach.
3. Mix cream cheese and Greek yogurt in a bowl. Add cheddar, parmesan, garlic powder and salt, stir well to combine.
4. Add spinach and stir well. Microwave the dip for 30 seconds and stir well. Serve with sliced veggies of choice.

ZUCCHINI MINI PIZZAS

Cooking time : 20 minutes - **Servings:** 24

INGREDIENTS:

- 1 zucchini, cut into 1/4 inch-slices
- 1/3 cup pizza sauce
- 3/4 cup mozzarella cheese, shredded
- 1/2 cup miniature pepperoni slices
- Minced fresh basil
- Salt, pepper, to taste

DIRECTIONS

1. Preheat broiler. Place zucchini slices in a single layer on a greased baking sheet.
2. Broil for 1-2 minutes per side.
3. Sprinkle zucchini with salt and pepper, top with sauce, cheese and pepperoni. Broil for about 1 minute. Serve topped with basil.

SHRIKHAND

Cook time: 10 minutes + chilling time - **Servings:** 2

INGREDIENTS:

- 3/4 cup Greek yogurt
- 2 tablespoons Erythritol
- few strands saffron crushed into mortar and pestle
- 1 teaspoon milk
- 1/4 teaspoon green cardamom seeds powder
- 4-5 cashew nuts chopped finely

- 4-5 almonds chopped finely
- 4-5 pistachios chopped finely, optional

DIRECTIONS

1. Dissolve crushed saffron in the warm milk.
2. Put Greek yogurt, Erythritol into a bowl and stir till everything is combined well.
3. Add saffron milk, cardamom powder, chopped nuts and mix well.
4. Put it into a refrigerator for couple of hours before serving.

BADAM KULFI

Cook time: 4 hours 20 minutes - **Servings:** 4

INGREDIENTS:

- 2 cups ground almonds, blanched & peeled
- 2 cups condensed milk
- 1/2 cup milk
- 8 tablespoons fresh cream
- 15 strand saffron
- 6 pieces pistachios
- 2 tablespoons blanched almonds

DIRECTIONS

1. Combine ground almonds, cream condensed milk in a large bowl and whisk until thick. Set aside.
2. Heat milk in a saucepan on a high flame and then boil it.
3. When milk starts boiling, add saffron strands and mix well. Then remove pan from the flame and let the mixture cool.
4. Once it cools, combine it with the almond mixture and stir well (the consistency should be creamy and thick).
5. Heat another pan on a moderate flame, add coarsely chopped pistachios, almonds and dry roast for a few seconds.
6. Once done, combine it with the kulfi mixture (reserve some for garnish), mix well and pour the mixture into the kulfi moulds.
7. Cover the top with a lid and keep in a freezer for 4 hours or until set.
8. Once done, remove kulfi from the mould and sprinkle with some of the reserved pistachios and almonds.

LAUKI KI KHEER

Cook time: 40 minutes - **Servings :** 6

INGREDIENTS:

- 2 tablespoons ghee

- 12 almonds, crushed

- 12 cashews, crushed

- 2 cups Lauki/Bottle gourd, grated

- 12 strands Saffron

- 2 tablespoons sweetener of choice

- 1 teaspoon Cardamom powder

DIRECTIONS

1. Preheat ghee in a pan over medium heat. Add almonds and cashews and fry until browned.

2. Add grated Lauki and fry for 5-6 minutes on low heat.

3. Add milk and bring everything to a boil. Reduce the heat to low and cook until the mixture thickens.

4. Add saffron and cook on low heat for 20-25 minutes, stirring from time to time.

5. Add cardamom powder and sweetener, cook for 3-4 minutes.

6. Serve topped with almond and pistachio slivers and rose petals. Serve chilled.

MUG MAIN MASTI

Cook time: 40 minutes - **Servings :** 6

INGREDIENTS:

- 2 tablespoons unsalted grass-fed butter

- 1 1/2 tablespoons cocoa powder

- 2 tablespoons erythritol

- 1 egg

- 2 tablespoons almond flour

- 1 tablespoon golden flaxseed meal

- 2 teaspoons coconut flour

- 1/2 teaspoon baking powder

- A pinch of salt

DIRECTIONS

1. Melt butter in a bowl. Add cocoa and sweetener, mix until well combined.

2. Add egg and mix until smooth. Add the remaining ingredients and pour the batter into a mug.

3. Place a paper towel into the microwave and place the mug on top. Cook on high for 70-90 seconds. Let cool for a couple minutes and enjoy!

CHICKPEA SUNDAL

Servings: 10

INGREDIENTS

- 2 tablespoons virgin coconut oil or vegetable oil
- 12 fresh curry leaves
- 6 dried kashmiri or guajillo chiles, broken into pieces, seeds removed
- 1 1/2 tablespoons black or brown mustard seeds
- 1/2 teaspoon asafetida (optional)
- 1/4 pound 15- can chickpeas, rinsed
- kosher salt
- 1/2 cup freshly grated coconut or unsweetened shredded coconut
- lime wedges (for serving)
- asafetida is a combination of dried gum resins from plant roots; available at indian markets.

DIRECTIONS

1. Warmth oil in a huge skillet over medium-high. Make mustard seeds, swirling pan sometimes until oil starts to sputter. Add curry leaves, chiles, and asafetida (if using) and prepare, stirring sometimes, until curry leaves are somewhat darkened about 45 mere seconds. Add chickpeas; make, tossing often, simply until warmed through, about three minutes. Let cool; time of year with salt.
2. Scoop Sunday right into a bowl; beat with coconut. Serve with lime wedges.

SLOW-COOKER CHICKEN TIKKA MASALA

Servings: 10

INGREDIENTS

- 2/3 cup plain greek yogurt
- 1 teaspoon ground coriander (optional)
- 4 pounds . boneless skinless chicken breasts, cut into 1" cubes
- kosher salt
- freshly ground black pepper
- 2 onions, chopped
- 2/3 cup garlic, minced
- 2 tablespoons freshly minced ginger
- 1 teaspoon ground turmeric
- 1 1/2 tablespoons ground cumin
- 1 1/2 tablespoons paprika

- 1 1/2 tablespoons garam masala

- 1 teaspoon cayenne pepper

- 2 cans 1 (28-oz.) crushed tomatoes

- 1 cup heavy cream

- kosher salt

- freshly chopped cilantro, for garnish

- rice or naan, for serving

DIRECTIONS

1. In the plate of the slow cooker, combine chicken, yogurt, and coriander; period with salt and pepper. Let marinate a quarter-hour. Mix in onion, garlic, ginger, and spices, after that add tomatoes. Cover and make until chicken is prepared through, on high for 4 hours or on low for 8 hours. Mix in cream and garnish with cilantro before serving.

SUSAN FENIGER

Servings: 10

INGREDIENTS

- 1/2 cup vegetable oil

- 2 1/2 pounds white onions, chopped

- 6 serrano chiles, sliced into rounds

- 2 2-inch-long piece fresh ginger, peeled, thinly sliced

- 8 garlic cloves, chopped

- 20 whole cloves

- 2 tablespoons cumin seeds

- 2 tablespoons ground cinnamon

- 1 1/2 tablespoons ground cardamom

- 2 teaspoons black peppercorns

- 15 cups (60 ounces) plain whole-milk yogurt, divided

- 3/4 cup fresh lemon juice

- 2 whole lamb shoulder (about 10 pounds), boned, trimmed of all fat (about 4 1/3 pounds)

- 3 tablespoons coarse kosher salt, divided

- 4 cups sliced almonds (about 7 ounces)

- 2 cups raw cashews (about 5 ounces)

- 1 cup (packed) golden brown sugar

- 2 tablespoons coarse kosher salt

DIRECTIONS

1. Heat oil in a large skillet over medium-high warmth. Add onions; sauté until golden, 14 moments. Add garlic and then 7 ingredients; stir 2 minutes. Scrape combination into the processor. Add 4 cups yogurt. Mix until mixture is usually coarse puree; transfer to a large bowl. Mix in 2 cups yogurt and lemon juice.

2. Place 1 glass yogurt marinade in normal size bowl. Cover, chill, and reserve for topping. Place 3 cups marinade in moderate bowl; mix in staying 1 1/2 cups yogurt and time of year with salt and pepper. Cover, chill, and reserve for sauce.

3. Place lamb in a large roasting pan and form into a rectangle approximately 12x6 ins (some slim layers may overlap). Sprinkle with 2 1/4 teaspoons salt; pass on with fifty percent of remaining marinade. Cautiously change lamb over. Sprinkle with staying 2 1/4 teaspoons salt; pass on with staying marinade. Cover with plastic material wrap. Refrigerate overnight.

4. Preheat oven to 375°F. Mix almonds, cashews, sugar, salt, and 1 glass marinade reserved for topping in processor chip until nuts are coarsely cut.

5. Remove plastic material and scrape the majority of the marinade off the best of lamb. Cover pan with foil and roast lamb for 1 1/2 hours. Uncover; pass on nut topping equally over. Roast lamb uncovered until topping is usually golden and lamb is usually tender about one hour. Let stand for ten minutes.

6. Transfer lamb to a platter. Serve, moving reserved sauce.

TELANGANA CHICKEN (TELANGANA-STYLE CURRIED CHICKEN STEW)

Servings: 4

INGREDIENTS

- 3 cups coconut milk
- 10 tbsp. plain, full-fat yogurt
- 2 tbsp. garam masala
- 2 teaspoons red chile powder, preferably kashmiri, or cayenne
- 3/4 cup garlic, peeled
- 6 tbsp. fresh lime juice
- 2 pieces 1 (4") ginger, peeled and thinly sliced
- kosher salt, to taste
- 6 pounds . chicken drumsticks and thighs, skin removed
- 54 fresh or frozen curry leaves, defrosted if frozen
- 16 green cardamom pods
- 2 pieces mace (optional)
- 2 star anise

- 1 cup cinnamon
- 1/2 cup canola or peanut oil
- 6 small green thai chiles or 1 1/2 serranos, halved
- 4 medium yellow onions, halved and thinly sliced crosswise
- 2 tbsp. chopped cilantro

DIRECTIONS

1. Purée coconut milk, yogurt, lime juice, garam masala, chile powder, garlic, ginger, and salt in a meals processor until clean; transfer to a bowl. Add poultry, 20 curry leaves, the cardamom, mace, if using, the celebrity anise, and cinnamon; toss to mix. Cover with plastic material wrap and chill overnight.
2. The very next day, heat oil within an 8-qt. saucepan over medium-high. Make chiles and onions until caramelized, about 20 minutes. Utilizing a slotted spoon, transfer combination to a bowl; reserve. Add poultry and its own marinade to pan; boil. Reduce heat to moderate; simmer until poultry is cooked through, about thirty minutes. Mix in chiles and onions; cook five minutes even more and garnish with cilantro and staying curry leaves.

SARA DICKERMAN

Servings: 10

INGREDIENTS

- 1/4 cup coconut or canola oil
- 2 teaspoons cumin seeds
- 6 garlic cloves, chopped
- 2 tablespoons finely chopped fresh ginger
- 2 teaspoons mustard seeds
- 2 medium onions, chopped
- fine sea salt
- 2 teaspoons ground turmeric
- pinch of cayenne pepper
- 4 large tomatoes, grated on a large grate, with juices reserved
- 2 1/2 pounds eggplant, cut into 1/2-inch cubes (about 5 cups)
- 2 ounces 15- can chickpeas, drained, rinsed, or 1 1/4 cups drained cooked chickpeas
- 2 1/2 tablespoons finely chopped jalapeño
- 2 shallots, finely chopped
- 2 tablespoons fresh lime juice, plus more
- 2 teaspoons honey
- 1/4 cup unsweetened flaked coconut

- 2 cups coarsely chopped mint leaves
- 1/2 cup coarsely chopped cilantro leaves
- freshly ground black pepper
- plain yogurt (for serving)

DIRECTIONS

1. Heat oil more than medium-high in a sizable skillet or Dutch oven. Add cumin and mustard seeds and prepare for 30 seconds, after that add garlic and ginger. Stir continuously until garlic just starts to brown, about 1 minute, then mix in onion and a generous pinch of salt. Cook, stirring often, until onion is normally tender, about five minutes. Mix in turmeric and cayenne. Pour in tomatoes and their juices, scraping up any browned bits with a wooden spoon. Add eggplant, chickpeas, ¼ cup drinking water, and a pinch of salt, mix and reduce high temperature to medium-low. Cover the pan and simmer until eggplant is normally tender, about a quarter-hour.
2. Remove from high temperature and increase jalapeño, shallot, lime juice, and honey. Fold in coconut, mint, and cilantro. Season to flavor with salt, dark pepper, and lime juice.
3. Best with a dollop of yogurt before serving.

ALAINA SULLIVAN

Servings: 10

INGREDIENTS

- 2 cups whole milk or unsweetened nut milk (such as hemp, almond, or cashew)
- 1 teaspoon ground turmeric
- 1/2 teaspoon ground ashwagandha (or another adaptogen, like shatavari or astralagus)
- 1 teaspoon ground cinnamon
- 1/4 teaspoon of ground cardamom
- pinch of ground ginger (optional)
- pinch of ground nutmeg
- freshly ground black pepper
- 2 teaspoons virgin coconut oils or ghee
- 2 teaspoons honey, preferably raw

DIRECTIONS

1. Bring milk to a simmer in a little saucepan over medium-low high temperature. Whisk in cinnamon, turmeric, ashwagandha, cardamom, ginger, if using, and nutmeg; period with pepper. Whisk vigorously to include any clumps. Add coconut essential oil, reduce high temperature to low, and continue steadily to make until warmed through, 5-10 minutes (the much longer you move, the more powerful the medication). Remove from high temperature and let cool somewhat. Stir in honey (you wish to avoid

cooking food honey or you'll destroy its curing goodness). Pour right into a mug, beverage warm, and climb directly into bed.

SPICE-MARINATED AND GRILLED LAMB CHOPS

Servings: 10

INGREDIENTS

- 1 teaspoon fennel seeds
- 2 2-inch piece ginger, peeled, finely grated
- 8 garlic cloves, finely grated
- 1/2 cup crème fraîche or sour cream
- 2 serrano chile, finely grated
- 1/4 cup fresh lime juice
- 2 tablespoons mustard oils (optional)
- 2 teaspoons dried mangos powder (amchoor; optional)
- 2 teaspoons dried fenugreek leaves
- 2 teaspoons freshly ground black pepper
- 1 teaspoon finely grated nutmeg
- 2 teaspoons kashmiri chili powder or paprika, plus more for serving
- 1/4 cup vegetable oil, plus more for grill
- 24 lamb rib chops (about 2 1/4 pounds total), frenched
- kosher salt
- leaf mint , cilantro leaves with tender stems, and lemons wedges (for serving)
- a spice mill or mortar and pestle

DIRECTIONS

1. Toast fennel seeds in a dried-out small skillet over moderate heat, shaking pan frequently, until fragrant, about 45 seconds; let great. Finely grind in a spice mill or with mortar and pestle. Transfer to a sizable bowl; add chile, ginger, garlic, crème fraîche, lime juice, mustard essential oil (if using), mango powder (if using), fenugreek leaves, pepper, nutmeg, 1 tsp. chili powder, and 2 Tbsp. vegetable essential oil and mix well. Period lamb chops with salt and increases marinade; turn to layer. Cover and chill for at least 2 hours.

2. Allow lamb chops to sit at area temperature one hour before grilling.

3. Make a grill for moderate heat; essential oil grate. Grill lamb to preferred doneness, about three minutes per aspect for medium-uncommon. Transfer to a platter; let rest 5-10 minutes.

4. Best lamb with mint and cilantro and dust with an increase of chili powder. Serve with lemon wedges.

5. Do Ahead: Lamb could be marinated 12 hours forward. Keep chilled.

ALISON ROMAN

Servings: 10

INGREDIENTS

- 1 1/2 cups whole milk
- 2 ounces 1/4- envelope active dry yeast
- 7 cups all-purpose flour plus more for surface and hands
- 2 teaspoons kosher salt plus more
- 2 teaspoons sugar
- 2 small onions, finely chopped
- 2 cups whole-milk yogurt (not greek)
- 1/4 cup melted ghee (clarified butter) or vegetable oil plus more

DIRECTIONS

1. Heat milk in a little saucepan over medium-low warmth until an instant-read thermometer registers 100°. Transfer to a little bowl and whisk in yeast and sugars. Allow standing until foamy, about ten minutes.
2. Whisk 3 1/2 cups flour and 1 teaspoon salt in a huge bowl to mix. Add yeast combination, onion, yogurt, and 2 tablespoons ghee. Blend dough until blended but nonetheless shaggy.
3. Transfer dough to a lightly floured function surface area. Knead until an easy dough forms, adding flour as required (dough will become sticky), about five minutes. Gently grease another large bowl with ghee, place dough in the bowl, and change to coating. Cover with plastic material wrap. Allow rise in a warm, draft-free region until doubled in proportions, about 1 hour.
4. Punch straight down dough and divide it into 10 items. Using floured hands, roll each piece right into a ball on a gently floured surface area. Cover with plastic material wrap; let rest ten minutes.
5. Heat a huge cast-iron or another heavy skillet over medium-high warmth. Lightly coating with ghee. Dealing with 1 piece at the same time, stretch dough together with your hands or roll out with a rolling pin to 1/8-in. thickness. Sprinkle with salt. Cook until gently blistered, puffed, and prepared through, about 2 minutes per part. Wrap in foil to maintain warm until prepared to serve.
6. Perform AHEAD: Naan dough could be produced 4 hours before shaping. Cover and chill.

SANDESH (BENGALI MILK SWEETS)

Servings: 4

INGREDIENTS

- 2 1/2 tablespoons fresh lemon juice

- 2 1/2 tablespoons sugar
- 4 cups whole milk
- 1/2 teaspoon ground cardamom
- golden raisins or shelled pistachios, for garnish

DIRECTIONS

1. Bring milk to a boil in a 6-qt. saucepan, stirring occasionally to avoid scorching. Add lemon juice and remove from temperature; large curds will form. Utilizing a wooden spoon, lightly push curds collectively toward one part of the pot; usually do not mix or the curd will break right into small pieces. Range a fine-mesh sieve with dampened cheesecloth; stress curds and discard whey or conserve for another make use of. Rinse curds under cool running water.

2. Gather edges of cheesecloth together to create a purse. Tie edges around a wooden spoon. Place the spoon over a huge pot, balancing ends of a spoon to ensure that purse hangs openly. Let drain at space temperature for one hour; discard any liquid that collects in the pot. Transfer purse to a colander and cover with a heavy-bottom pot filled up with drinking water; allow cheese drain one hour.

3. Unwrap cheese and transfer to a function surface area. Using hands, knead cheese until soft ball forms, 2-3 minutes. Steadily add sugar and cardamom; knead until smooth. Temperature a 12” nonstick skillet over medium. Make cheese mixture, stirring sometimes, until slightly dry, however, not golden, about ten minutes. Remove from temperature and let cool somewhat. Using hands, divide the dough into 8 balls. Press a golden raisin or pistachio into each ball.

ALOO AUR GOSHT KA KALIYA (HYDERABADI-STYLE LAMB WITH POTATOES)

Servings: 8

INGREDIENTS

- 2/3 cup olive oil
- 12 green cardamom pods
- 12 whole cloves
- 2 pounds . medium red potatoes, peeled and quartered
- 6 medium onions, halved and thinly sliced crosswise
- 4 pounds . bone-in lamb shoulder, cut into 2" pieces (ask your butcher)
- kosher salt, to taste
- 2 teaspoons red chile powder, preferably kashmiri, or cayenne
- 1 1/2 teaspoons ground turmeric

- 1/4 cup garlic, mashed into a paste
- 2 pieces 1 (1") ginger, peeled and grated
- 2 cups plain, full-fat yogurt
- 1 1/2 cups minced cilantro
- 2 tbsp. pumpkins seeds, ground in a spice grinder
- 6 small green thai chiles, or 1 serrano, halved
- 1 teaspoon garam masala

DIRECTIONS

1. Heat oil in an 8-qt. saucepan over medium-high. Produce potatoes until golden, 10-12 minutes; employing a slotted spoon, transfer to a bowl. Add cardamom and cloves to pan; cook until fragrant, about 1 minute. Add onions; cook until relatively caramelized, about 20 occasions. Transfer onions to bowl with potatoes. Season lamb with salt; make, turning simply because required, until browned, 8-10 occasions. Add chile powder, turmeric, garlic, and ginger; make 1 minute. Add yogurt 1/4 glass simultaneously and stirring occasionally until lamb mixture is thick and relatively dry, 10-12 occasions. Add 2 cups normal water; boil. Reduce warmth to medium-low; make, protected, until lamb is certainly tender, about 1 hour. Mix in reserved potatoes and onions, the cilantro, flooring pumpkin seeds, chiles, and salt. Mix softly to mix and offer to a simmer once more. Simmer until potatoes are tender, about quarter-hour a lot more. Mix in garam masala before serving.

SOUTH INDIAN CURRY-MASHED POTATOES (ALOO MASALA)

Servings: 8

INGREDIENT

- 4 pounds . yukon gold potatoes
- 1/2 cup canola oil
- 1 teaspoon asafoetida
- 1 teaspoon fenugreek seeds
- 2 teaspoons black mustard seeds
- 40 fresh or frozen curry leaves
- 1/2 cup garlic, chopped
- 6 small green thai chiles or 1 serrano, halved
- 2 large yellow onions, roughly chopped
- 1 cup frozen peas
- 3 tbsp. ground coriander

- 2 teaspoons ground turmeric
- 2 (2-inch) piece ginger, peeled and grated
- kosher salt, to taste
- 2/3 cup chopped cilantro

DIRECTIONS

1. Make potatoes in boiling drinking water until just tender, 25-30 a few minutes; drain, peel, and trim into 2" pieces. High-temperature oil in a 6-qt. saucepan over medium-high. Make mustard seeds until they pop, 1-2 a few minutes. Add asafoetida, fenugreek seeds, and curry leaves; make 1 minute. Add garlic, chiles, and onion; prepare until golden, 8-10 a few minutes. Add potatoes, peas, coriander, turmeric, ginger, salt, and 1/2 glass water; boil. Reduce high temperature to medium-low; cook, protected, until potatoes are tender, 8-10 a few minutes. Uncover and mix, mashing gently; cook until slightly dried out, 4-5 minutes. Mix in cilantro.

SAMOSAS (FRIED POTATO-FILLED PASTRIES)

Servings: 12

INGREDIENTS

- 1 1/2 cups flour
- 4 tbsp. unsalted butter, cubed and chilled
- kosher salt, to taste
- 1/4 pound . russet potatoes, peeled and roughly chopped
- 1 carrot, roughly chopped
- 6 tablespoons ice-cold water
- 1 tbsp. canola oil, plus more
- 1/2 teaspoon cumin seeds
- 1/2 small yellow onion, minced
- 6 tablespoons frozen peas, defrosted
- 2 tablespoons minced cilantro
- 2 tablespoons minced mint
- 1/4 teaspoon garam masala
- 1 small green thai chiles or 1 serrano, minced
- 1/2 piece 1 (1") of ginger, peeled and minced
- tamarind and coconut-cilantro chutneys, for serving (optional)

DIRECTIONS

1. Make the dough: Pulse flour, butter, and salt in a food processor chip into pea-size crumbles. Add drinking water; pulse until dough forms. Divide into 12 balls; chill one hour.

2. Make the filling: Boil potatoes and carrots in a 4-qt. a saucepan of salted drinking water until tender, 8-10 a few minutes. Drain; coarsely mash. Add 2 tbsp. essential oil to pan; high temperature over medium-high. Make cumin seeds until they pop, 1-2 a few minutes. Add onion and ginger; cook until golden, 4-6 minutes. Let great; stir into potato mix with peas, cilantro, mint, garam masala, chiles, and salt.

3. Type and fry samosas: Dealing with 1 ball at the same time, roll the dough right into a 6" circular; cut in two. Gather direct edges of just one 1 half-round jointly, overlapping by 1/4" to create a cone. Moisten seam with drinking water; press to seal. Spoon 1 tbsp. filling into cone. Moisten edges of a cone with drinking water; pinch to seal. High temperature 2" essential oil in a 6-qt. saucepan until a deep-fry thermometer reads 350°. Fry samosas until sharp, 8-10 minutes. Drain in some recoverable format towels; serve with chutneys if you want.

ALOO GOBI

Servings: 10

INGREDIENTS

- 1/4 cup vegetable oil
- 2 red chili, diced
- 2 tablespoons minced ginger
- 2 teaspoons garam masala
- 1/4 cup garlic, minced
- 1 teaspoon dried turmeric
- 1/2 teaspoon cayenne pepper
- 6 russets, peeled and chopped into 1" pieces
- 2 medium head cauliflower, cut into florets
- 2 cups low-sodium vegetable broth
- kosher salt
- freshly ground black pepper
- freshly chopped cilantro, for serving

DIRECTIONS

1. In a huge skillet over medium-high heat, heat oil. Add chili, garlic, and ginger and prepare until fragrant, 1 minute. Add garam masala, turmeric, and cayenne and prepare until toasted, 1 minute even more. Add potatoes, cauliflower, and vegetable broth and time of year with salt and pepper. Reduce heat and make, protected, until potatoes and cauliflower are tender, quarter-hour. Garnish with cilantro to provide.

CARLA LALLI MUSIC

Servings: 10

INGREDIENTS

- 2 1/2-inch piece fresh ginger, unpeeled, coarsely grated
- 1/4 cup loose strong black tea or 6 tea bags (such as tips)
- 28 green cardamom pods, lightly crushed, or 3/4 teaspoon cardamom seeds, lightly crushed
- 2 3-inch cinnamon sticks, lightly crushed with the flat side of a knife
- 5 1/2 cups milk
- 1/2 cup pure maple syrup

DIRECTIONS

1. Bring ginger, cinnamon, and 3½ cups normal water to a boil in an average saucepan on a lot more than medium-high high temperature. Decrease warmth and simmer quickly, stirring occasionally, until liquid is reduced by a third and intensely fragrant, about 20 minutes.
2. Remove pan from warmth, mix in tea and cardamom, and permit steep 2 minutes.
3. Keep coming back pan to medium-high warmth and combine in milk and maple syrup. Cook, stirring occasionally and keeping a close watch until mixture begins to foam up and boil about 5 minutes. Immediately remove from warmth and allow sit for 5 minutes. Tension chai through a fine-mesh sieve into a teapot or pitcher and offer.

BABY BACK RIBS WITH TAMARIND GLAZE

Servings: 10

INGREDIENTS

- 4 racks pork ribs baby back pork ribs (3½–4 pounds total) halved crosswise
- 2 oranges orange wedge (about ⅛ of orange)
- 10 star anise pods
- 2/3 pound ginger ginger peeled chopped
- 4 cups apple juice unfiltered apple juice
- 2 tablespoons salt Diamond Crystal or 2 teaspoons Morton kosher salt
- 12 habanero chiles halved lengthwise seeds removed if desired divided
- cup light brown sugar ¼ plus ⅓ (lightly packed) light brown sugar
- cup ketchup ½ ketchup
- cup cider vinegar ⅓ apple cider vinegar

- cup ¼ tamarind concentrate
- 6 tablespoons honey honey
- vegetable oil Vegetable oil (for grill)
- salt Kosher salt
- 2 cucumbers Persian cucumber thinly sliced
- red onion ½ small red onion thinly sliced
- serrano chile ½ serrano chile very thinly sliced
- 1 1/2 tablespoons lime juice fresh lime juice
- sprig cilantro Micro cilantro and/or cilantro and lime wedges (for serving)
- can Often labeled "concentrate cooking tamarind" or "paste" tamarind concentrate be found at Asian markets and online.

DIRECTIONS

1. Place ribs in a sizable Dutch oven or various other large pots. Add ginger, orange wedge, superstar anise, apple juice, salt, fifty percent of chiles, and ¼ glass dark brown sugar. Pour in drinking water merely to cover pork and provide to a simmer over moderate heat. Reduce heat therefore liquid is at an extremely mild simmer, partially cover the pot, and braise, turning racks several times until meats are fork-tender and almost (however, not quite) dropping off the bones, 1½-2 hours. Chop staying chiles while ribs are cooking food and set aside.

2. Cautiously transfer ribs to a rimmed baking sheet and let cool. Cut between ribs to produce 2-rib pieces.

3. Meanwhile, crank up the heat beneath the Dutch oven to high and put ketchup, vinegar, tamarind focus, honey, remaining ⅓ cup dark brown sugar, and reserved chopped chiles to braising liquid. Cook, stirring frequently until glaze is solid enough to coat a spoon (it must be reduced to 1-1½ cups), 30-45 minutes. Stress into a huge measuring glass; discard solids. Allow settle so essential oil rises to the surface area. Pour off essential oil into a little bowl; set aside.

4. Do Ahead: Ribs could be braised one day ahead. Let awesome in liquid; cover and chill.

5. Make a grill for moderate heat; oil grate. Functioning individually, dip ribs into the glaze to coating. Grill ribs, turning many times, until glaze is usually lightly charred, about five minutes total. Transfer ribs to a platter; time of year with salt. Drizzle with staying glaze and reserved essential oil.

6. Toss cucumber, onion, chile, and lime juice in a moderate bowl to combine; time of year with salt. Scatter salad over ribs and best with micro cilantro. Serve with lime wedges.

CHEDDAR CHEESE-STUFFED KULCHA

Servings: 10

INGREDIENTS

- 1 teaspoon dry active yeast

- 8 cups plus 3 tbsp. (1 1/4 lb.) all-purpose flour, plus more for dusting
- 1 1/2 tablespoons . fine sea salt, divided
- 2 tbsp. plus 1/2 tsp. sugar, divided
- 2 tbsp. canola oils, plus more for greasing
- 8 cups (1 lb.) grated cheddar
- 2 large red bell pepper, finely diced (1 cup)
- 2 tbsp. ground cumin
- 1 teaspoon cayenne pepper
- melted ghee, for brushing
- tomato tadka or chutney, for serving (optional)

DIRECTIONS

1. In the bowl of a stand mixer installed with a dough hook, combine the yeast with 1/2 teaspoon sugar and 1 tablespoon plus 1 1/2 teaspoons lukewarm water. Reserve prior to the yeast provides helped type little bubbles at the top of the water, about five minutes.

2. Add 1 1/4 cups of cold water to the yeast mixture, accompanied simply by the flour, keeping sugar, and 2 1/4 teaspoons salt. Blend on the cheapest velocity until a dough begins to create, 3-3 1/2 occasions. At the moment, if all the flour isn't hydrated and the dough appears extremely dry, add 1-2 extra tablespoons of cold water and mix on low velocity for 30 seconds a lot more. Increase to the next velocity and combine before dough is simple and elastic, 2 occasions more. Decrease the velocity once more, add the canola gas, and mix prior to the oil is equally integrated and the dough is normally homogenous, 2-3 occasions. (The dough should be very sticky and simple, but very smooth.)

3. Lightly oil a medium bowl with canola oil. Transfer the dough to the bowl, turning it over many times to thoroughly covering with the essential oil. Cover the bowl firmly with plastic material and reserve at space temperature before dough is usually inflated, extremely gassy, and nearly doubled in proportions, 80-90 minutes.

4. Generously dust a clean countertop with flour and switch the dough away from any of it. Divide the dough into 5 comparatives (6-oz.) items, softly rounding each into a ball.

5. Lightly oil an enormous baking sheet with canola oil place the dough rounds at the very top, spacing them similarly. Cover tightly with plastic-type material wrap and refrigerate for at least 8 hours or even more to 2 days.

6. One hour before you'll be prepared to bake, preheat a pizza organic stone in a 500° oven. In a moderate bowl, combine the cheese, bell pepper, cumin, cayenne, and remaining 1/4 teaspoon salt; reserve.

7. When the rock is heated, generously flour a countertop. Get rid of the dough from the refrigerator and place among the balls of dough on the floured surface (cover all of those other balls with a clean towel or sheet of the plastic-type material wrap in order to avoid them from blow drying when you work). Make usage of a rolling pin to flatten one little dough out to a 10-in. circle. Pile 1 cup of cheese

completing a concise mound at the guts of the circle, from then on pleat the sides up to meet at the guts to seal the cheese within the pouch of dough. Continue filling all those additional balls. Allow stand at least 30 mins before rolling out the kulcha. (Alternately, you can cover and refrigerate the stuffed balls overnight.)

8. Working separately, lightly flour the kulcha, flatten gently, then roll again away to even 8-inches rounds. (If any atmosphere bubbles are trapped within, slit the dough with the finish of a sharpened knife, deflate the bubble, and pinch the beginning back again jointly to seal.) Repeat with all of that other kulcha.

9. Working quickly to make sure that the oven won't lose temperature among loading, utilize the hands or a pizza peel to transfer 2-3 3 kulchas to your pizza rock. (Bake as many pieces as a possible match on the rock without overlapping or crowding.) Immediately close the oven and bake 5-7 mins, until it truly is irregularly puffed and browned in areas underneath and the cheese within is obviously thoroughly melted.

10. Make usage of a spatula or pizza peel to remove the kulcha and transfer it to a clean baking sheet. Brush softly with ghee and cover with a dry out towel when you keep up baking all that other kulcha.

11. Serve warm, fundamental, or with tomato tadka or chutney privately.

ANDY BARAGHANI

Servings: 10

INGREDIENTS

- 16 scallions (about 1 bunch), divided
- 6 garlic cloves, smashed
- 2 3-inch piece ginger, peeled, smashed to pieces, thinly sliced
- 8 skinless, boneless chicken breasts (about 2 1/4 pounds)
- 1/4 cup mild curry powder
- 2 tablespoons diamond crystal or 1 3/4 teaspoons morton kosher salt, divided, plus more
- juice from 1 orange (about 1/4 cup)
- juice from 1 lime (about 2 tablespoons)
- freshly ground black pepper
- warm jasmine rice (for serving)

DIRECTIONS

1. Coarsely chop 4 scallions and transfer to a medium pot. Add chicken, garlic, ginger, curry powder, 2½ tsp. salt, and 4 cups water. Gradually provide to a bare simmer over moderate heat. Once the liquid starts to simmer, reduce the warmth to low and make until juices run obviously when the thickest component of chicken is definitely pierced, 10-12 minutes.

2. Meanwhile, thinly slice the remaining scallions. Whisk orange juice and lime juice in a little bowl; time of year with salt and 8 turns of a pepper mill, or around ¾ tsp. (you will want a large amount of pepper!).

3. Transfer chicken to a cutting plank and let great slightly. Stress poaching liquid through a fine-mesh sieve into a little bowl. Cut chicken crosswise into slim slices.

4. Divide rice and chicken among bowls and best with sliced scallions. Spoon poaching liquid plus some of the citrus juice over chicken and rice before serving.

5. Do Ahead: Chicken could be poached 2 days forward. Allow chicken and curry great individually. Wrap chicken and transfer curry to an airtight container; chill.

JOANNA CISMARU

Servings: 8

INGREDIENTS

- 2 cups   chickpeas drained
- 2 teaspoons   smoked paprika
- 2 teaspoons garlic powder
- 1/2 teaspoon salt or to taste
- 2 teaspoons cumin
- 1 teaspoon pepper or to taste
- 2   large cauliflower broken into florets
- 2 teaspoons cumin ground
- 2 teaspoons   garam masala *
- 1 teaspoon salt
- 1 teaspoon   ground turmeric **
- 1/2 teaspoon cayenne pepper
- 4 chicken breasts boneless and skinless cut in 1 inch cubes
- 1/4 cup olive oil
- 1/4 cup garlic minced
- 2 teaspoons   fresh ginger grated
- 2   small onions chopped
- 2 cups carrots shredded
- 2 cups peas frozen
- 1/4 cup cilantro for garnish

DIRECTIONS

1. Preheat oven to 400 F degrees. Spray a baking sheet with cooking spray.

2. In a moderate bowl toss jointly the chickpeas with the smoked paprika, cumin, garlic powder, salt, and pepper. Make certain each chickpea is protected in spices. Pass on the chickpeas within an even level over the ready baking sheet.

3. Roast the chickpeas in the oven for approximately 20 to thirty minutes or until dry out and crispy externally.

4. Meanwhile, place the cauliflower florets in a food processor chip and pulse until the blend resembles the consistency of rice. You will likely want to do this in a few batches. Place in a bowl and reserve.

5. In a moderate bowl combine the cumin, garam masala, salt, turmeric, and cayenne pepper. Add the poultry parts and toss and make certain each poultry piece is covered in the spice blend.

6. In a sizable wok or skillet heat 1 tbsp of the essential olive oil over moderate-high heat. Add the minced garlic and ginger and make for 10 secs. Add the poultry to the wok and make for approximately 5 to 6 mins or before the chicken is no pinker and begins to brown a little bit. Stir as necessary to ensure the poultry cooks on all sides.

7. Remove the poultry from the wok. Add the rest of the 1 tbsp of essential olive oil and add onion, carrots, and peas. Make and stir for 2 mins. Add the cauliflower rice and stir well, after that cook for another 4 mins until cauliflower can be tender. Period with salt and pepper if required. Return poultry to work and temperature through.

8. Serve even though warm topped with the roasted chickpeas and cilantro.

INDIAN LENTIL STEW (KHATTI DAL)

Servings: 8

INGREDIENTS

- 2 cups toor dal (yellow pigeon peas), rinsed, soaked 30 minutes, and drained
- 1/2 teaspoon ground turmeric
- 2 teaspoons tamarind paste
- 1/2 teaspoon red chile powder, such as cayenne
- 6 tbsp. chopped cilantro
- 24 fresh or frozen curry leaves
- 1 cup garlic (1 mashed into a paste, 6 peeled)
- 4 plum tomatoes, peeled and minced
- 4 small green thai chiles, or 1 serrano, thinly sliced
- 2 (1/2-inch) piece ginger, peeled and grated
- kosher salt, to taste
- 6 tbsp. canola oil
- 1 teaspoon cumin seeds

- 1/2 teaspoon brown mustard seeds
- 6 chiles de árbol

DIRECTIONS

1. Bring dal and 8 cups drinking water to a boil in a 6-qt. saucepan. Reduce heat to moderate; mix in the turmeric and prepare until dal is definitely mushy about 45 minutes.
2. Mix in cilantro, tamarind paste, chile powder, curry leaves, garlic paste, tomatoes, sliced chiles, ginger, and salt; boil. Reduce warmth to moderate; cook until somewhat thickened, about quarter-hour.
3. Heat oil within an 8" skillet more than medium-high. Make cumin and mustard seeds until they pop, 1-2 moments. Add peeled garlic and the chiles de árbol; cook until garlic is definitely golden, 6-8 moments, and mix into the stew.

KACHI YAKHNI BIRYANI (HYDERABADI-STYLE STEAMED CHICKEN AND RICE)

Servings: 12

INGREDIENTS

- 2 cups canola oil
- 2 large yellow onions, thinly sliced
- 2 cups roughly chopped cilantro
- 2 cups roughly chopped mint
- 2 (3 1/2-4-lb.) chicken, cut into 8 pieces
- 6 tbsp. garam masala
- 2 teaspoons red chile powder, such as cayenne
- 1/2 teaspoon ground turmeric
- 3/4 cup garlic, peeled
- 4 small green thai chiles or 1 serrano, stemmed
- 2 pieces 1 (4") ginger, peeled and thinly sliced
- juice of half a lemon
- kosher salt, to taste
- 4 cups plain, full-fat yogurt
- 1 teaspoon kala jerra (black cumin seeds)
- 6 whole cloves
- 4 green cardamom pods
- 1 cup cinnamon
- 4 cups long-grain white rice

- 1 cup ghee, melted

DIRECTIONS

1. Heat 1 cup essential oil and the onion in a 6-qt. saucepan over medium heat. Make, stirring sometimes, until onion is certainly caramelized, about 25 minutes; utilizing a slotted spoon, transfer onion to a bowl and reserve essential oil for another use.

2. Cut chicken into 18 pieces: Cut poultry into 8 pieces, discarding wingtips. Cut each drumstick, thigh, and wing in two and cut each breast crosswise into 3 parts; transfer to a bowl.

3. Purée 1/3 the reserved onion, the cilantro, mint, garam masala, chile powder, turmeric, garlic, green chiles, ginger, lemon juice, and salt in a little food processor right into a paste; arranged half the paste apart. Add staying paste to the bowl with poultry. Add yogurt; toss to mix. Cover with plastic material wrap; chill one hour.

4. Clean pan clean and put cumin, cloves, cardamom, cinnamon, and 6 cups drinking water; boil. Mix in rice; prepare until rice is somewhat tender, about five minutes. Stress rice and spices, discarding drinking water. Spoon 1/3 the rice and spice combination into pan; best with half the poultry and its own marinade. Sprinkle with fifty percent the rest of the herb paste, drizzle with 1/3 the ghee, and sprinkle 1/3 the rest of the onion over top. Do it again layering the rest of the rice, poultry, herb paste, and ghee. Steam, protected, on low warmth until rice and poultry are completely cooked, 35-40 moments. Garnish with staying caramelized onion.

INDIAN LIME RICE

Servings: 8

INGREDIENTS

- 2 cups basmati rice, rinsed until water runs clear
- 3 tbsp. chana dal (yellow split peas), rinsed until water runs clear
- 1/2 cup canola oil
- 1/2 teaspoon ground turmeric
- 24 fresh or frozen curry leaves
- 2 teaspoons black mustard seeds
- 1/2 cup garlic, thinly sliced
- 8 small green thai chiles or 2 serranos, roughly chopped
- 1/2 teaspoon asafoetida
- 1/2 cup fresh lime juice
- kosher salt, to taste

DIRECTIONS

1. Bring 6 cups of drinking water to a boil in a 4-qt. saucepan. Add rice; make, stirring sometimes, until

rice is certainly tender, 10-12 a few minutes. Meanwhile, combine dal and 1 cup drinking water in a bowl; allow sit 30 minutes, after that drain. Drain the rice and transfer to a bowl. Add essential oil to pan; high temperature over medium-high. Make mustard seeds until they pop, 1-2 a few minutes. Add reserved dal; prepare until reddish-brown, 5-7 a few minutes. Add turmeric, curry leaves, garlic, and chiles; prepare until garlic is certainly golden, 2-3 a few minutes. Add asafoetida; stir into rice with lime juice and salt.

MAACHER JHOL (BENGALI-STYLE FISH STEW)

Servings: 8

INGREDIENTS

- 2 pounds . boneless, skin-on catfish, trout, or salmon, cut into 2" pieces
- 1/2 teaspoon ground turmeric
- kosher salt, to taste
- 3 tbsp. black mustard seeds
- 2 tbsp. cumin seeds
- 2/3 cup mustard oils
- 1 1/2 tablespoons panch phoran (bengali five-spice powder)
- 4 small green thai chiles or 1 serrano, halved
- 6 tablespoons garlic, mashed into a paste
- 2 pieces 1 (2") ginger, peeled and mashed into a paste
- 2 small red onions, minced
- 4 plum tomatoes, chopped
- 2/3 cup packed cilantro leaves

DIRECTIONS

1. Rub seafood with turmeric and salt in a bowl. Warmth a 6-qt. saucepan over medium-high; make mustard and cumin seeds until they pop, 1-2 moments. Grind in a spice grinder right into a powder. Add essential oil to pan; warmth over medium-high. Cook seafood, flipping once, until pores and skin are crisp, 4-5 moments; transfer to a plate. Add five-spice powder and chiles; cook 1-2 moments. Add onion; prepare until somewhat caramelized, 8-10 moments. Add reserved spices, garlic, ginger, and 1 1/2 cups drinking water; boil. Add tomatoes; prepare until thickened, 8-10 minutes. Stir in seafood and the cilantro.

INDIAN SPICED CHICKPEA FLATBREAD

{SOCCA}

Servings: 4

INGREDIENTS

- 2 cups chickpea or garbanzo bean flour
- 2 cups water
- 6 tablespoons + 2 teaspoons extra virgin olive oils divided
- 1 teaspoon ground coriander
- 1/2 teaspoon ground turmeric
- 1 teaspoon salt
- 1/4 - 1/4 teaspoon cayenne pepper
- 1 medium yellow onion chopped
- 2/3 cup diced tomatoes
- 2 garlic cloves minced
- 1/4 cup minced cilantro

DIRECTIONS

1. In a moderate bowl, whisk jointly the chickpea flour, water, 1 tablespoon plus 1 teaspoon essential olive oil, salt, ground coriander, and turmeric.
2. Cover with plastic material wrap and allow mixture rest at area temperature for at least 2 hours.
3. Preheat the broiler, with the rack set 7 to 8 in . from the element.
4. High temperature 1 teaspoon of essential olive oil in a sizable nonstick skillet place over medium-high heat.
5. Add the onion and prepare until needs to brown, about 2 minutes. Mix in the tomato and prepare for three minutes. Add the garlic and make for 30 seconds. Mix the vegetables into the chickpea flour batter.
6. Place a huge (10-in .) cast-iron skillet in the oven to preheat for five minutes.
7. Using an oven mitt or potholder, carefully take away the cast iron skillet from the oven. Pour in 1 tablespoon essential olive oil and swirl to coating the pan.
8. Pour in two of the batter and instantly swirl to coat underneath the pan.
9. Place beneath the broiler and make until the best and edges are beginning to blacken and blister, four to six 6 minutes.
10. Cautiously transfer the flatbread to a cutting board, cut into 8 wedges, garnish with cilantro and serve.
11. Repeat with the rest of the 1 tablespoon essential olive oil, butter, and cilantro.

MALIKA MASOOR DAL (RED LENTILS WITH GREEN MANGO

Servings: 4

INGREDIENTS

- 1 cup masoor dal (split red lentils), rinsed, soaked 30 minutes, and drained
- 1/2 tbsp. ground turmeric
- 3 amchoor slices (dried, green mango)
- 1/2 piece 1 (1") ginger, peeled and mashed into a paste
- 1/2 cup garlic (3 mashed into a paste, 12 peeled)
- kosher salt, to taste
- 1 1/2 tbsp. ghee
- 1 chiles de árbol, chopped
- 1 1/2 tbsp. roughly chopped cilantro, for garnish

DIRECTIONS

1. Bring dal, turmeric, garlic paste, the anchor slices, ginger paste, salt, and 6 cups drinking water to a boil in a 6-qt. saucepan. Reduce heat to moderate; cook, covered somewhat, until dal is normally mushy, about 20 minutes. Utilizing a whisk, vigorously mix dal until even and creamy.
2. Melt ghee within an 8" skillet over medium-high heat. Make peeled garlic and the chiles until golden, 4-5 a few minutes, and pour over dal; garnish with cilantro.

INSTANT POT BUTTER CHICKEN

Servings: 10

INGREDIENTS

- 2 tablespoons vegetable oil
- 2 tablespoons butter
- 1 1/2 tablespoons freshly grated ginger
- 2/3 cup garlic, crushed and roughly chopped
- 2 large onions, diced
- 2 cans 1 (6-oz.) tomato paste
- 4 pounds . boneless skinless chicken thighs, cut into 1" pieces
- 2 tablespoons garam masala
- 2 teaspoons paprika
- 2 tablespoons granulated sugar
- 2 teaspoons ground cumin
- 1 teaspoon turmeric
- kosher salt
- freshly ground black pepper

- 1 1/2 cups heavy cream
- rice, for serving
- naan, for serving
- yogurt, for serving
- cilantro, for serving

DIRECTIONS

1. Preheat Quick Pot to Sauté environment. Once heated, add essential oil and butter after that add onion, ginger, and garlic. Allow sear until gently browned, three to four 4 mins. Add tomato paste and make, mixing continuously until it really is darkened in color, about three minutes. Add 1/2 cup water, poultry, and spices to the pot, and time of year with salt and pepper. Seal lid and arranged to Pressure Make on High for five minutes. Let pressure launch naturally for ten minutes and follow the manufacturer's guidelines for quick releasing staying steam. Stir in weighty cream and modify seasoning with salt and pepper. Serve with rice, naan, yogurt, and cilantro.

KASHMIRI HOT SAUCE

Servings: 10

INGREDIENTS

- 1 teaspoon fennel seeds
- 1/2 teaspoon black or brown mustard seeds
- 10 fresh red chiles (such as fresno)
- 1/4 cup distilled white vinegar
- 2 medium tomatoes, halved crosswise, seeds removed
- 2 teaspoons kashmiri chili powder or paprika
- 2 teaspoons kosher salt
- 1 teaspoon sugar
- a spice mill or mortar and pestle

DIRECTIONS

1. Toast fennel seeds and mustard seeds in a dried-out small saucepan over moderate heat, shaking pan frequently, until fragrant, about 45 mere seconds. Transfer to a plate and allow awesomely. Finely grind in a spice mill or with mortar and pestle. Transfer back again to pan.
2. Pulse tomato and chiles in a meals processor until the fine floor. Transfer to a saucepan with floor spices and blend in vinegar, chili powder, salt, and sugar. Bring to a simmer over moderate heat, stirring often; prepare until chiles are gentle and sauce is somewhat thickened, 5-7 a few minutes. Let cool.
3. Do Forward: Hot sauce could be made 1 week forward. Cover and chill.

INSTANT POT INDIAN BUTTER SHRIMP

Servings: 8

INGREDIENTS

- 1/2 cup plain whole-milk yogurt
- 1 1/2 tablespoons ground cumin
- 1 1/2 tablespoons garam masala
- 1 1/2 tablespoons lime juice
- 1 1/2 tablespoons sweet paprika
- 1 tablespoon kosher salt
- 2 teaspoons freshly grated ginger, use a microplane if you have one
- 2 garlic cloves, grated with a microplane or minced
- 4 pounds large shrimp, peeled and deveined
- 1/2 cup butter, divided
- 4 shallots, minced
- 4 garlic cloves, grated or minced
- 1 tablespoon grated fresh ginger
- 2 teaspoon crushed red pepper flakes
- 1/2 teaspoon kosher salt
- 2 (28-ounce) cans diced tomatoes, with juice
- 2 cups heavy cream
- 1 teaspoon finely grated limes zest
- cooked basmati rice
- chopped fresh cilantro

DIRECTIONS

1. In a moderate bowl, mix jointly yogurt, cumin, paprika, garam masala, lime juice, salt, ginger, and garlic to create a marinade. Mix in shrimp. Refrigerate for a quarter-hour to at least one 1 hour.

2. While shrimp is marinating, prepare the sauce. Convert Quick Pot to "saute" and add 2 tablespoons butter.

3. Once the butter has melted, combine shallots and a pinch of salt. Make until golden brown, four to six 6 minutes.

4. Mix in garlic, ginger, crimson pepper flakes, and 1/4 teaspoon salt and cook another one to two 2 minutes.

5. Mix in tomatoes and their juice, large cream, and another pinch of salt. Bring the mix to a boil. After that cover and place on ruthless for 8 a few minutes. Make certain valve is considered "sealing". Discharge the pressure manually. When the pin drops, take away the lid.

6. Turn on the "saute" setting and simmer the sauce to thicken about 4 to 7 a few minutes.

7. Mix in the shrimp and marinade, the rest of the 2 tablespoons butter, and the lime zest and make 2 to five minutes, or until shrimp are pink, being careful never to overcook. They will continue steadily to make in the sauce once you take them off from the moment Pot.

8. Serve with rice and cilantro.

QUICK CHICKEN CURRY

Serves: 4-6 - **Preparation Time:** 5 minutes - **Cooking time:** 15-20 minutes

INGREDIENTS

- 2-3 pounds cooked chicken, poached or roasted
- 1 ½ tablespoons mustard or vegetable oil
- 1 small onion, thinly sliced
- 1 teaspoon ginger, grated
- 3 cloves garlic, minced
- 1 tablespoon curry powder
- ½-1 teaspoon red chili flakes
- 1 medium tomato, diced
- ½ cup yogurt
- 1 (14-ounce) can coconut milk
- 1-2 pieces bay leaf
- ½ teaspoon salt, or to taste
- ¼ teaspoon black pepper
- ½ teaspoon sugar (optional)
- ¼ cup fresh cilantro leaves, roughly chopped
- 1 cup white rice

DIRECTIONS

1. shred the pre-cooked chicken, or cut it into bite-sized pieces.

2. heat the oil in a frying pan or wok over medium-high heat and sauté the onions and ginger until fragrant and the onion is tender (about 5-8 minutes).

3. add garlic and sauté about a minute longer until fragrant.

4. add the chicken and stir-fry. for roast chicken pieces, heat through. if you're using poached chicken, cook until slightly browned.

5. add the curry powder, chili flakes and tomato. stir-fry for about 3 minutes, or until the tomatoes are slightly mushy.

6. reduce the heat to medium-low and add yogurt, coconut milk, bay leaves, black pepper, salt, and sugar

(optional). stir and simmer until thickened, about 3-5 minutes.

7. adjust the seasoning and spices, if desired.
8. remove from the heat, sprinkle with cilantro, and serve with rice or naan.

CHICKEN MADRAS

Serves: 4 - **Preparation Time:** 30 minutes - **Cooking time:** 30 minutes to 1 hour

INGREDIENTS

- 4 boneless skinless chicken breasts or thighs, cut into bite-sized pieces

For marinade:

- 1 ½ tablespoons freshly squeezed lemon juice
- 1 teaspoon garam masala
- Salt, to taste

For sauce:

- 2 tablespoons ghee or vegetable oil
- 1 large onion, finely chopped
- 3-5 tablespoons Madras curry paste
- 1 (16-ounce) can chopped tomatoes
- ½ cup desiccated coconut

For garnish:

- ¼ cup fresh cilantro, chopped

DIRECTIONS

1. combine the ingredients for the marinade and toss in the chicken pieces. set aside.
2. heat the oil in a karahi/wok, or frying pan. sauté the onion until it is almost golden in color (5-8 minutes).
3. add the chicken and cook for 5 minutes, stirring constantly.
4. add the madras paste and stir to distribute the flavor, than cook for 2 more minutes.
5. add the tomato and coconut, cover, and let it simmer for 20 minutes. the chicken should be cooked through.
6. add more salt or madras paste, if desired.
7. garnish with cilantro and serve with rice or naan.

BUTTER CHICKEN (MURGH MAKHAN)

Serves: 6 - **Preparation Time:** 15 minutes - **Cooking time:** 45 minutes

INGREDIENTS

- 1 cup butter, divided

- 1 onion, minced
- 1 tablespoon minced garlic
- 1 ½ pounds boneless skinless chicken breast, cut into bite-sized chunks
- 2 tablespoons vegetable oil
- 2 tablespoons tandoori masala
- 1 (15-ounce) can tomato sauce
- 3 cups heavy cream
- 2 teaspoons salt
- 1 teaspoon cayenne pepper
- 1 teaspoon garam masala

DIRECTIONS

1. preheat the oven to 375°f.
2. take about 2 tablespoons of the butter and melt it in a karahi (or any skillet) over medium heat.
3. add the onion and garlic and cook for 15 minutes, stirring occasionally, or until the onion becomes dark brown in color.
4. in a bowl, combine the chicken with the oil and toss to coat. add the tandoori masala and mix well.
5. arrange the chicken pieces in one layer on a baking sheet.
6. bake for about 12 minutes, or until the chicken is thoroughly cooked.
7. in another pan, melt the rest of the butter over medium-high heat.
8. stir in the tomato sauce, cream, salt, cayenne, and garam masala.
9. reduce the heat to medium low and simmer for 30 minutes.
10. add the caramelized onion and the baked chicken, and simmer for 5 minutes.

GOAN FISH CURRY

Serves: 4-6 - **Preparation Time:** 15 minutes - **Cooking time:** 20-30 minutes

INGREDIENTS

- 2 tablespoons vegetable oil
- 1 large onion, finely chopped
- 4 large cloves fresh garlic, minced
- 1 cup water
- 1 teaspoon salt, or to taste
- 1 cup coconut milk
- 2-3 tablespoons tamarind paste
- 1 ½ pounds fish fillets, 1 inch thick, cut into 2-inch pieces
- ¼ cup finely chopped fresh cilantro, including soft stems

For spice mix:

- 3 dried red chili peppers, broken into pieces
- 1 teaspoon coriander seeds
- 1 teaspoon cumin seeds
- ¼ teaspoon ground turmeric

DIRECTIONS

1. grind together the red chili peppers, coriander, cumin, and turmeric in a small spice grinder. set aside.
2. heat the oil in a large nonstick wok or saucepan over medium-high heat and stir-fry the onion for 5 minutes or until golden.
3. add the garlic and stir 1 minute, then stir in the spice mixture and cook 2 minutes more.
4. pour in the water and coconut milk. bring to a boil, stirring constantly. reduce the heat and simmer for 5 minutes.
5. add the tamarind paste and salt. stir well.
6. add the fish and continue simmering for 10-15 minutes, or until the fish is opaque and easy to flake with a fork.
7. sprinkle with cilantro and serve.

FISH SKEWERS (FISH TANDOORI TIKKA)

Serves: 4 - Preparation Time: 10 minutes plus 8 hours and 10 minutes marinating time - **Cooking time:** 15 minutes

INGREDIENTS

- 1 ½ pounds fish fillets, cut into 1 ½-inch cubes

For first marinade:

- Salt, to taste
- ⅛ teaspoon red chili powder
- 4 tablespoons freshly squeezed lemon juice

For second marinade:

- 1 cup yogurt
- ½ teaspoon garam masala
- ¼ teaspoon red chili powder
- ¼ teaspoon cumin powder
- ¼ teaspoon pepper powder
- 2 cloves garlic, minced
- 1 teaspoon ginger, minced

For garnish:

- Pinch of chaat masala
- Lemon wedges

DIRECTIONS

1. wipe the fish with paper towels to dry.
2. gently rub the ingredients for the first marinade all over the fish. cover, and refrigerate for 10 minutes.
3. in a bowl, combine ingredients for second marinade.
4. gently massage the mixture onto the fish and let it marinate for 6-8 hours.
5. skewer the fish pieces and grill for about 7-8 minutes on each side.
6. sprinkle with chaat masala and serve with wedges of lemon.

MIXED SEAFOOD CURRY

Serves: 6 - **Preparation Time:** 20 minutes - **Cooking time:** 15 minutes

INGREDIENTS

- 2 tablespoons vegetable oil
- 1 medium onion, halved and sliced
- 1 tablespoon ginger, minced
- 1 tablespoon garlic, minced
- 2-3 pieces green chili
- ½ teaspoon red chili powder (optional)
- ½ teaspoon turmeric powder
- 1 (14-ounce) can light coconut milk
- 3 tablespoons lime juice
- 1 tablespoons curry powder, or according to taste
- 1 tablespoon brown sugar
- 12 medium shrimp, peeled (tails left on) and deveined
- 12 sea scallops, halved
- 2 tablespoons chopped cilantro
- Salt to taste

DIRECTIONS

1. heat oil in a karahi/kadai or wok over medium-high heat.
2. sauté the onion until tender, about 2-3 minutes.
3. stir in the ginger, garlic, and green chili, and sauté until fragrant, about 1 minute.
4. add red chili powder (optional), turmeric, coconut milk, lime juice, curry powder, and brown sugar. bring to a simmer and cook for 5 minutes.
5. add the shrimp, scallops, cilantro, and salt, and cook until the shrimps and scallops become opaque,

about 5 minutes.

6. adjust the flavor with more salt and spices if needed.

JOANNA CISMARU

Servings: 8

INGREDIENTS

- 2 cups   chickpeas drained
- 2 teaspoons   smoked paprika
- 2 teaspoons garlic powder
- 1/2 teaspoon salt or to taste
- 2 teaspoons cumin
- 1 teaspoon pepper or to taste
- 2   large cauliflower broken into florets
- 2 teaspoons cumin ground
- 2 teaspoons   garam masala *
- 1 teaspoon salt
- 1 teaspoon   ground turmeric **
- 1/2 teaspoon cayenne pepper
- 4 chicken breasts boneless and skinless cut in 1 inch cubes
- 1/4 cup olive oil
- 1/4 cup garlic minced
- 2 teaspoons   fresh ginger grated
- 2   small onions chopped
- 2 cups carrots shredded
- 2 cups peas frozen
- 1/4 cup cilantro for garnish

DIRECTIONS

1. Preheat oven to 400 F degrees. Spray a baking sheet with cooking spray.

2. In a moderate bowl toss jointly the chickpeas with the smoked paprika, cumin, garlic powder, salt, and pepper. Make certain each chickpea is protected in spices. Pass on the chickpeas within an even level over the ready baking sheet.

3. Roast the chickpeas in the oven for approximately 20 to thirty minutes or until dry out and crispy externally.

4. Meanwhile, place the cauliflower florets in a food processor chip and pulse until the blend resembles the consistency of rice. You will likely want to do this in a few batches. Place in a bowl and reserve.

5. In a moderate bowl combine the cumin, garam masala, salt, turmeric, and cayenne pepper. Add the poultry parts and toss and make certain each poultry piece is covered in the spice blend.

6. In a sizable wok or skillet heat 1 tbsp of the essential olive oil over moderate-high heat. Add the minced garlic and ginger and make for 10 secs. Add the poultry to the wok and make for approximately 5 to 6 mins or before the chicken is no pinker and begins to brown a little bit. Stir as necessary to ensure the poultry cooks on all sides.

7. Remove the poultry from the wok. Add the rest of the 1 tbsp of essential olive oil and add onion, carrots, and peas. Make and stir for 2 mins. Add the cauliflower rice and stir well, after that cook for another 4 mins until cauliflower can be tender. Period with salt and pepper if required. Return poultry to work and temperature through.

8. Serve even though warm topped with the roasted chickpeas and cilantro.

INDIAN LENTIL STEW (KHATTI DAL)

Servings: 8

INGREDIENTS

- 2 cups toor dal (yellow pigeon peas), rinsed, soaked 30 minutes, and drained
- 1/2 teaspoon ground turmeric
- 2 teaspoons tamarind paste
- 1/2 teaspoon red chile powder, such as cayenne
- 6 tbsp. chopped cilantro
- 24 fresh or frozen curry leaves
- 1 cup garlic (1 mashed into a paste, 6 peeled)
- 4 plum tomatoes, peeled and minced
- 4 small green thai chiles, or 1 serrano, thinly sliced
- 2 (1/2-inch) piece ginger, peeled and grated
- kosher salt, to taste
- 6 tbsp. canola oil
- 1 teaspoon cumin seeds
- 1/2 teaspoon brown mustard seeds
- 6 chiles de árbol

DIRECTIONS

1. Bring dal and 8 cups drinking water to a boil in a 6-qt. saucepan. Reduce heat to moderate; mix in the turmeric and prepare until dal is definitely mushy about 45 minutes.

2. Mix in cilantro, tamarind paste, chile powder, curry leaves, garlic paste, tomatoes, sliced chiles, ginger, and salt; boil. Reduce warmth to moderate; cook until somewhat thickened, about quarter-hour.

3. Heat oil within an 8" skillet more than medium-high. Make cumin and mustard seeds until they pop, 1-2 moments. Add peeled garlic and the chiles de árbol; cook until garlic is definitely golden, 6-8 moments, and mix into the stew.

KACHI YAKHNI BIRYANI (HYDERABADI-STYLE STEAMED CHICKEN AND RICE)

Servings: 12

INGREDIENTS

- 2 cups canola oil
- 2 large yellow onions, thinly sliced
- 2 cups roughly chopped cilantro
- 2 cups roughly chopped mint
- 2 (3 1/2-4-lb.) chicken, cut into 8 pieces
- 6 tbsp. garam masala
- 2 teaspoons red chile powder, such as cayenne
- 1/2 teaspoon ground turmeric
- 3/4 cup garlic, peeled
- 4 small green thai chiles or 1 serrano, stemmed
- 2 pieces 1 (4") ginger, peeled and thinly sliced
- juice of half a lemon
- kosher salt, to taste
- 4 cups plain, full-fat yogurt
- 1 teaspoon kala jerra (black cumin seeds)
- 6 whole cloves
- 4 green cardamom pods
- 1 cup cinnamon
- 4 cups long-grain white rice
- 1 cup ghee, melted

DIRECTIONS

1. Heat 1 cup essential oil and the onion in a 6-qt. saucepan over medium heat. Make, stirring sometimes, until onion is certainly caramelized, about 25 minutes; utilizing a slotted spoon, transfer onion to a bowl and reserve essential oil for another use.

2. Cut chicken into 18 pieces: Cut poultry into 8 pieces, discarding wingtips. Cut each drumstick, thigh, and wing in two and cut each breast crosswise into 3 parts; transfer to a bowl.

3. Purée 1/3 the reserved onion, the cilantro, mint, garam masala, chile powder, turmeric, garlic, green chiles, ginger, lemon juice, and salt in a little food processor right into a paste; arranged half the paste apart. Add staying paste to the bowl with poultry. Add yogurt; toss to mix. Cover with plastic material wrap; chill one hour.

4. Clean pan clean and put cumin, cloves, cardamom, cinnamon, and 6 cups drinking water; boil. Mix in rice; prepare until rice is somewhat tender, about five minutes. Stress rice and spices, discarding drinking water. Spoon 1/3 the rice and spice combination into pan; best with half the poultry and its own marinade. Sprinkle with fifty percent the rest of the herb paste, drizzle with 1/3 the ghee, and sprinkle 1/3 the rest of the onion over top. Do it again layering the rest of the rice, poultry, herb paste, and ghee. Steam, protected, on low warmth until rice and poultry are completely cooked, 35-40 moments. Garnish with staying caramelized onion.

INDIAN LIME RICE

Servings: 8

INGREDIENTS

- 2 cups basmati rice, rinsed until water runs clear
- 3 tbsp. chana dal (yellow split peas), rinsed until water runs clear
- 1/2 cup canola oil
- 1/2 teaspoon ground turmeric
- 24 fresh or frozen curry leaves
- 2 teaspoons black mustard seeds
- 1/2 cup garlic, thinly sliced
- 8 small green thai chiles or 2 serranos, roughly chopped
- 1/2 teaspoon asafoetida
- 1/2 cup fresh lime juice
- kosher salt, to taste

DIRECTIONS

1. Bring 6 cups of drinking water to a boil in a 4-qt. saucepan. Add rice; make, stirring sometimes, until rice is certainly tender, 10-12 a few minutes. Meanwhile, combine dal and 1 cup drinking water in a bowl; allow sit 30 minutes, after that drain. Drain the rice and transfer to a bowl. Add essential oil to pan; high temperature over medium-high. Make mustard seeds until they pop, 1-2 a few minutes. Add reserved dal; prepare until reddish-brown, 5-7 a few minutes. Add turmeric, curry leaves, garlic, and chiles; prepare until garlic is certainly golden, 2-3 a few minutes. Add asafoetida; stir into rice with lime juice and salt.

MAACHER JHOL (BENGALI-STYLE FISH STEW)

Servings: 8

INGREDIENTS

- 2 pounds . boneless, skin-on catfish, trout, or salmon, cut into 2" pieces
- 1/2 teaspoon ground turmeric
- kosher salt, to taste
- 3 tbsp. black mustard seeds
- 2 tbsp. cumin seeds
- 2/3 cup mustard oils
- 1 1/2 tablespoons panch phoran (bengali five-spice powder)
- 4 small green thai chiles or 1 serrano, halved
- 6 tablespoons garlic, mashed into a paste
- 2 pieces 1 (2") ginger, peeled and mashed into a paste
- 2 small red onions, minced
- 4 plum tomatoes, chopped
- 2/3 cup packed cilantro leaves

DIRECTIONS

1. Rub seafood with turmeric and salt in a bowl. Warmth a 6-qt. saucepan over medium-high; make mustard and cumin seeds until they pop, 1-2 moments. Grind in a spice grinder right into a powder. Add essential oil to pan; warmth over medium-high. Cook seafood, flipping once, until pores and skin are crisp, 4-5 moments; transfer to a plate. Add five-spice powder and chiles; cook 1-2 moments. Add onion; prepare until somewhat caramelized, 8-10 moments. Add reserved spices, garlic, ginger, and 1 1/2 cups drinking water; boil. Add tomatoes; prepare until thickened, 8-10 minutes. Stir in seafood and the cilantro.

INDIAN SPICED CHICKPEA FLATBREAD {SOCCA}

Servings: 4

INGREDIENTS

- 2 cups chickpea or garbanzo bean flour
- 2 cups water
- 6 tablespoons + 2 teaspoons extra virgin olive oils divided

- 1 teaspoon ground coriander
- 1/2 teaspoon ground turmeric
- 1 teaspoon salt
- 1/4 - 1/4 teaspoon cayenne pepper
- 1 medium yellow onion chopped
- 2/3 cup diced tomatoes
- 2 garlic cloves minced
- 1/4 cup minced cilantro

DIRECTIONS

1. In a moderate bowl, whisk jointly the chickpea flour, water, 1 tablespoon plus 1 teaspoon essential olive oil, salt, ground coriander, and turmeric.
2. Cover with plastic material wrap and allow mixture rest at area temperature for at least 2 hours.
3. Preheat the broiler, with the rack set 7 to 8 in . from the element.
4. High temperature 1 teaspoon of essential olive oil in a sizable nonstick skillet place over medium-high heat.
5. Add the onion and prepare until needs to brown, about 2 minutes. Mix in the tomato and prepare for three minutes. Add the garlic and make for 30 seconds. Mix the vegetables into the chickpea flour batter.
6. Place a huge (10-in .) cast-iron skillet in the oven to preheat for five minutes.
7. Using an oven mitt or potholder, carefully take away the cast iron skillet from the oven. Pour in 1 tablespoon essential olive oil and swirl to coating the pan.
8. Pour in two of the batter and instantly swirl to coat underneath the pan.
9. Place beneath the broiler and make until the best and edges are beginning to blacken and blister, four to six 6 minutes.
10. Cautiously transfer the flatbread to a cutting board, cut into 8 wedges, garnish with cilantro and serve.
11. Repeat with the rest of the 1 tablespoon essential olive oil, butter, and cilantro.

MALIKA MASOOR DAL (RED LENTILS WITH GREEN MANGO)

Servings: 4

INGREDIENTS

- 1 cup masoor dal (split red lentils), rinsed, soaked 30 minutes, and drained
- 1/2 tbsp. ground turmeric
- 3 amchoor slices (dried, green mango)
- 1/2 piece 1 (1") ginger, peeled and mashed into a paste
- 1/2 cup garlic (3 mashed into a paste, 12 peeled)

- kosher salt, to taste
- 1 1/2 tbsp. ghee
- 1 chiles de árbol, chopped
- 1 1/2 tbsp. roughly chopped cilantro, for garnish

DIRECTIONS

1. Bring dal, turmeric, garlic paste, the anchor slices, ginger paste, salt, and 6 cups drinking water to a boil in a 6-qt. saucepan. Reduce heat to moderate; cook, covered somewhat, until dal is normally mushy, about 20 minutes. Utilizing a whisk, vigorously mix dal until even and creamy.

2. Melt ghee within an 8" skillet over medium-high heat. Make peeled garlic and the chiles until golden, 4-5 a few minutes, and pour over dal; garnish with cilantro.

INSTANT POT BUTTER CHICKEN

Servings: 10

INGREDIENTS

- 2 tablespoons vegetable oil
- 2 tablespoons butter
- 1 1/2 tablespoons freshly grated ginger
- 2/3 cup garlic, crushed and roughly chopped
- 2 large onions, diced
- 2 cans 1 (6-oz.) tomato paste
- 4 pounds . boneless skinless chicken thighs, cut into 1" pieces
- 2 tablespoons garam masala
- 2 teaspoons paprika
- 2 tablespoons granulated sugar
- 2 teaspoons ground cumin
- 1 teaspoon turmeric
- kosher salt
- freshly ground black pepper
- 1 1/2 cups heavy cream
- rice, for serving
- naan, for serving
- yogurt, for serving
- cilantro, for serving

DIRECTIONS

1. Preheat Quick Pot to Sauté environment. Once heated, add essential oil and butter after that add onion,

ginger, and garlic. Allow sear until gently browned, three to four 4 mins. Add tomato paste and make, mixing continuously until it really is darkened in color, about three minutes. Add 1/2 cup water, poultry, and spices to the pot, and time of year with salt and pepper. Seal lid and arranged to Pressure Make on High for five minutes. Let pressure launch naturally for ten minutes and follow the manufacturer's guidelines for quick releasing staying steam. Stir in weighty cream and modify seasoning with salt and pepper. Serve with rice, naan, yogurt, and cilantro.

KASHMIRI HOT SAUCE

Servings: 10

INGREDIENTS

- 1 teaspoon fennel seeds
- 1/2 teaspoon black or brown mustard seeds
- 10 fresh red chiles (such as fresno)
- 1/4 cup distilled white vinegar
- 2 medium tomatoes, halved crosswise, seeds removed
- 2 teaspoons kashmiri chili powder or paprika
- 2 teaspoons kosher salt
- 1 teaspoon sugar
- a spice mill or mortar and pestle

DIRECTIONS

1.Toast fennel seeds and mustard seeds in a dried-out small saucepan over moderate heat, shaking pan frequently, until fragrant, about 45 mere seconds. Transfer to a plate and allow awesomely. Finely grind in a spice mill or with mortar and pestle. Transfer back again to pan.

2. Pulse tomato and chiles in a meals processor until the fine floor. Transfer to a saucepan with floor spices and blend in vinegar, chili powder, salt, and sugar. Bring to a simmer over moderate heat, stirring often; prepare until chiles are gentle and sauce is somewhat thickened, 5-7 a few minutes. Let cool.

3. Do Forward: Hot sauce could be made 1 week forward. Cover and chill.

INSTANT POT INDIAN BUTTER SHRIMP

Servings: 8

INGREDIENTS

- 1/2 cup plain whole-milk yogurt
- 1 1/2 tablespoons ground cumin
- 1 1/2 tablespoons garam masala

- 1 1/2 tablespoons lime juice
- 1 1/2 tablespoons sweet paprika
- 1 tablespoon kosher salt
- 2 teaspoons freshly grated ginger, use a microplane if you have one
- 2 garlic cloves, grated with a microplane or minced
- 4 pounds large shrimp, peeled and deveined
- 1/2 cup butter, divided
- 4 shallots, minced
- 4 garlic cloves, grated or minced
- 1 tablespoon grated fresh ginger
- 2 teaspoon crushed red pepper flakes
- 1/2 teaspoon kosher salt
- 2 (28-ounce) cans diced tomatoes, with juice
- 2 cups heavy cream
- 1 teaspoon finely grated limes zest
- cooked basmati rice
- chopped fresh cilantro

DIRECTIONS

1. In a moderate bowl, mix jointly yogurt, cumin, paprika, garam masala, lime juice, salt, ginger, and garlic to create a marinade. Mix in shrimp. Refrigerate for a quarter-hour to at least one 1 hour.
2. While shrimp is marinating, prepare the sauce. Convert Quick Pot to "saute" and add 2 tablespoons butter.
3. Once the butter has melted, combine shallots and a pinch of salt. Make until golden brown, four to six 6 minutes.
4. Mix in garlic, ginger, crimson pepper flakes, and 1/4 teaspoon salt and cook another one to two 2 minutes.
5. Mix in tomatoes and their juice, large cream, and another pinch of salt. Bring the mix to a boil. After that cover and place on ruthless for 8 a few minutes. Make certain valve is considered "sealing". Discharge the pressure manually. When the pin drops, take away the lid.
6. Turn on the "saute" setting and simmer the sauce to thicken about 4 to 7 a few minutes.
7. Mix in the shrimp and marinade, the rest of the 2 tablespoons butter, and the lime zest and make 2 to five minutes, or until shrimp are pink, being careful never to overcook. They will continue steadily to make in the sauce once you take them off from the moment Pot.
8. Serve with rice and cilantro.

QUICK CHICKEN CURRY

Serves: 4-6 **- Preparation Time:** 5 minutes **- Cooking time:** 15-20 minutes

INGREDIENTS

- 2-3 pounds cooked chicken, poached or roasted
- 1 ½ tablespoons mustard or vegetable oil
- 1 small onion, thinly sliced
- 1 teaspoon ginger, grated
- 3 cloves garlic, minced
- 1 tablespoon curry powder
- ½-1 teaspoon red chili flakes
- 1 medium tomato, diced
- ½ cup yogurt
- 1 (14-ounce) can coconut milk
- 1-2 pieces bay leaf
- ½ teaspoon salt, or to taste
- ¼ teaspoon black pepper
- ½ teaspoon sugar (optional)
- ¼ cup fresh cilantro leaves, roughly chopped
- 1 cup white rice

DIRECTIONS

1. shred the pre-cooked chicken, or cut it into bite-sized pieces.
2. heat the oil in a frying pan or wok over medium-high heat and sauté the onions and ginger until fragrant and the onion is tender (about 5-8 minutes).
3. add garlic and sauté about a minute longer until fragrant.
4. add the chicken and stir-fry. for roast chicken pieces, heat through. if you're using poached chicken, cook until slightly browned.
5. add the curry powder, chili flakes and tomato. stir-fry for about 3 minutes, or until the tomatoes are slightly mushy.
6. reduce the heat to medium-low and add yogurt, coconut milk, bay leaves, black pepper, salt, and sugar (optional). stir and simmer until thickened, about 3-5 minutes.
7. adjust the seasoning and spices, if desired.
8. remove from the heat, sprinkle with cilantro, and serve with rice or naan.

CHICKEN MADRAS

Serves: 4 **- Preparation Time:** 30 minutes **- Cooking time:** 30 minutes to 1 hour

INGREDIENTS

- 4 boneless skinless chicken breasts or thighs, cut into bite-sized pieces

For marinade:

- 1 ½ tablespoons freshly squeezed lemon juice
- 1 teaspoon garam masala
- Salt, to taste

For sauce:

- 2 tablespoons ghee or vegetable oil
- 1 large onion, finely chopped
- 3-5 tablespoons Madras curry paste
- 1 (16-ounce) can chopped tomatoes
- ½ cup desiccated coconut

For garnish:

- ¼ cup fresh cilantro, chopped

DIRECTIONS

1. combine the ingredients for the marinade and toss in the chicken pieces. set aside.
2. heat the oil in a karahi/wok, or frying pan. sauté the onion until it is almost golden in color (5-8 minutes).
3. add the chicken and cook for 5 minutes, stirring constantly.
4. add the madras paste and stir to distribute the flavor, than cook for 2 more minutes.
5. add the tomato and coconut, cover, and let it simmer for 20 minutes. the chicken should be cooked through.
6. add more salt or madras paste, if desired.
7. garnish with cilantro and serve with rice or naan.

BUTTER CHICKEN (MURGH MAKHAN)

Serves: 6 - **Preparation Time:** 15 minutes - **Cooking time:** 45 minutes

INGREDIENTS

- 1 cup butter, divided
- 1 onion, minced
- 1 tablespoon minced garlic
- 1 ½ pounds boneless skinless chicken breast, cut into bite-sized chunks
- 2 tablespoons vegetable oil
- 2 tablespoons tandoori masala
- 1 (15-ounce) can tomato sauce
- 3 cups heavy cream

- 2 teaspoons salt
- 1 teaspoon cayenne pepper
- 1 teaspoon garam masala

DIRECTIONS

1. preheat the oven to 375°f.
2. take about 2 tablespoons of the butter and melt it in a karahi (or any skillet) over medium heat.
3. add the onion and garlic and cook for 15 minutes, stirring occasionally, or until the onion becomes dark brown in color.
4. in a bowl, combine the chicken with the oil and toss to coat. add the tandoori masala and mix well.
5. arrange the chicken pieces in one layer on a baking sheet.
6. bake for about 12 minutes, or until the chicken is thoroughly cooked.
7. in another pan, melt the rest of the butter over medium-high heat.
8. stir in the tomato sauce, cream, salt, cayenne, and garam masala.
9. reduce the heat to medium low and simmer for 30 minutes.
10. add the caramelized onion and the baked chicken, and simmer for 5 minutes.

GOAN FISH CURRY

Serves: 4-6 - **Preparation Time:** 15 minutes - **Cooking time:** 20-30 minutes

INGREDIENTS

- 2 tablespoons vegetable oil
- 1 large onion, finely chopped
- 4 large cloves fresh garlic, minced
- 1 cup water
- 1 teaspoon salt, or to taste
- 1 cup coconut milk
- 2-3 tablespoons tamarind paste
- 1 ½ pounds fish fillets, 1 inch thick, cut into 2-inch pieces
- ¼ cup finely chopped fresh cilantro, including soft stems

For spice mix:

- 3 dried red chili peppers, broken into pieces
- 1 teaspoon coriander seeds
- 1 teaspoon cumin seeds
- ¼ teaspoon ground turmeric

DIRECTIONS

1. grind together the red chili peppers, coriander, cumin, and turmeric in a small spice grinder. set aside.

2. heat the oil in a large nonstick wok or saucepan over medium-high heat and stir-fry the onion for 5 minutes or until golden.

3. add the garlic and stir 1 minute, then stir in the spice mixture and cook 2 minutes more.

4. pour in the water and coconut milk. bring to a boil, stirring constantly. reduce the heat and simmer for 5 minutes.

5. add the tamarind paste and salt. stir well.

6. add the fish and continue simmering for 10-15 minutes, or until the fish is opaque and easy to flake with a fork.

7. sprinkle with cilantro and serve.

FISH SKEWERS (FISH TANDOORI TIKKA)

Serves: 4 - Preparation Time: 10 minutes plus 8 hours and 10 minutes marinating time - **Cooking time:** 15 minutes

INGREDIENTS

- 1 ½ pounds fish fillets, cut into 1 ½-inch cubes

For first marinade:

- Salt, to taste
- ⅛ teaspoon red chili powder
- 4 tablespoons freshly squeezed lemon juice

For second marinade:

- 1 cup yogurt
- ½ teaspoon garam masala
- ¼ teaspoon red chili powder
- ¼ teaspoon cumin powder
- ¼ teaspoon pepper powder
- 2 cloves garlic, minced
- 1 teaspoon ginger, minced

For garnish:

- Pinch of chaat masala
- Lemon wedges

DIRECTIONS

1. wipe the fish with paper towels to dry.

2. gently rub the ingredients for the first marinade all over the fish. cover, and refrigerate for 10 minutes.

3. in a bowl, combine ingredients for second marinade.

4. gently massage the mixture onto the fish and let it marinate for 6-8 hours.

5. skewer the fish pieces and grill for about 7-8 minutes on each side.

6. sprinkle with chaat masala and serve with wedges of lemon.

MIXED SEAFOOD CURRY

Serves: 6 - **Preparation Time:** 20 minutes - **Cooking time:** 15 minutes

INGREDIENTS

- 2 tablespoons vegetable oil
- 1 medium onion, halved and sliced
- 1 tablespoon ginger, minced
- 1 tablespoon garlic, minced
- 2-3 pieces green chili
- ½ teaspoon red chili powder (optional)
- ½ teaspoon turmeric powder
- 1 (14-ounce) can light coconut milk
- 3 tablespoons lime juice
- 1 tablespoons curry powder, or according to taste
- 1 tablespoon brown sugar
- 12 medium shrimp, peeled (tails left on) and deveined
- 12 sea scallops, halved
- 2 tablespoons chopped cilantro
- Salt to taste

DIRECTIONS

1. heat oil in a karahi/kadai or wok over medium-high heat.

2. sauté the onion until tender, about 2-3 minutes.

3. stir in the ginger, garlic, and green chili, and sauté until fragrant, about 1 minute.

4. add red chili powder (optional), turmeric, coconut milk, lime juice, curry powder, and brown sugar. bring to a simmer and cook for 5 minutes.

5. add the shrimp, scallops, cilantro, and salt, and cook until the shrimps and scallops become opaque, about 5 minutes.

6. adjust the flavor with more salt and spices if needed.

www.ingramcontent.com/pod-product-compliance
Lightning Source LLC
Chambersburg PA
CBHW081944160726
47999CB00008B/2501